Provecho

PROVECHO

**100 VEGAN MEXICAN RECIPES to
CELEBRATE CULTURE and COMMUNITY**

EDGAR CASTREJÓN

WITH SUSAN CHOUNG

TEN SPEED PRESS
California | New York

Contents

Introduction

If there's food on the table, you'll hear most Latinos say, "Provecho!" Like the French expression "bon appétit," a declaration of provecho is exchanged before a meal or said to someone who's partaking in one. Yet, somehow, *provecho* conveys more than just, "Enjoy your meal." It comes from the Spanish word *aprovechar* ("to make the most of"). It imparts a sense of joy, an appreciation for community, and gratitude for all that we share.

It's those same sentiments that I want to express through the recipes, stories, and photos in *Provecho*. This book celebrates and honors the traditional family recipes of my childhood while happily embracing a plant-based lifestyle that prioritizes health and well-being. The recipes on these pages are driven by nostalgia yet are distinctive and eminently doable. They will inspire both vegans and plant-curious eaters alike to explore the vibrant flavors of plant-based Mexican food.

I'm a proud first-generation Mexican American. In 1989, my parents left Tacámbaro, in the Mexican state of Michoacán, to start a new life north of the border. I was born and raised in a diverse neighborhood in Oakland, California, that I lovingly call "El Barrio." As with most Mexican families, everything in my home revolved around food. My passion for cooking (and eating!) was passed down to me by my family, like the eyebrows I inherited from my mom's side. I was weaned on fragrant beef stews and grilled meat, chicken tamales, and seafood ceviche. I also grew up on the food of my neighbors, who were from other Latin countries, such as Colombia and El Salvador.

Meat-centric dishes are a cornerstone of Mexican culture. Every gathering seemed to be a carnivore's delight, with huge platters of guiso with carne and nopales, sancocho (soup with a bunch of meat), tacos with marinated meats, and the like. I was always served meat at the dinner table; but at a certain point in my childhood, I started pushing it away from my plate. Looking back, maybe it's because I was forced to kill chickens with my uncle for meals. I never enjoyed it and, to be honest, the experience traumatized me. I eventually turned vegetarian in my early twenties. I never thought I could be vegan, though—I just loved cheese too much! Little did I know back then of the soul-satisfying alternatives to dairy that were available.

It was when I left home that I ventured into a plant-based lifestyle. College is where I completely changed the way I cook and enjoy food. I was the first person in my family to even attend college. I graduated from Chico State in 2017 with a bachelor's degree in horticulture and plant science. Learning about nutrition and how food impacts our bodies gave me a new perspective on how to eat. However, the true aha moment came when I was looking after the cows on the college grounds one day as part of my campus job. I came to see them as loving creatures, each one with a personality. They craved human contact and enjoyed being petted. It was then, in January 2016, that I vowed never to eat any animal products again.

Beyond the ethical reasons, I realized that going vegan was the ultimate gateway for me to express both my creativity and my knowledge of nutrition and cooking. (People also assume I'm a raw-food specialist, but I chose @edgarraw as my handle on social media to express my "raw" self.) The health benefits can't be underestimated either. I have plenty of family members who struggle with obesity, diabetes, or cardiovascular diseases. I was battling my own weight problems back then too. Even if I couldn't convince my relatives to completely give up animal products, I wanted to show them that eating more plant-based food is better for you and so delicious. And I hope I can convince others as well.

That's when I really set out to veganize the foods I grew up eating. However, I didn't want to call foods out for being vegan. I just wanted to make tasty food that happens to be plant-based. To make it compelling, I knew I had to bring the rich, comforting flavors of those formative cuisines with me. In my family, recipes have been passed down through generations, but not through recipe cards or in any written form. Instead, they're acquired through las manos magicas—an innate passion and understanding for the dish to be prepared. I was lucky enough to discover that I had "the magic hands" at a young age. When I was seventeen years old, I was cooking guisado de papa for relatives coming over. I must have done a really good job because people were teasing me, saying, "You can get married now!" That's something they would usually tell a woman who has real culinary chops. I took it as a compliment that I could make someone happy with food. Having las manos magicas has shaped so much of who I am today as an artist and self-taught chef.

As a child, I loved taking pictures of nature. Eventually, I was shooting food during my journey to eating healthier. It was also a way to show people how beautiful plant-based food can be and entice them to try it. Documenting my life and food in images has helped me remember everything.

Growing up, I spent hours in the kitchen, nurtured by the creative women in my family. In Mexican culture, as in many cultures around the world, women are the guardians of generational recipes. I cherish those memories of helping mi mama, tias, and abuelita prepare the dishes they had previously helped their mothers, aunts, and grandmothers make. As a child, I loved the food that we cooked together. But as I got older, my body and soul craved a different way of eating.

Adopting a vegan lifestyle was a game changer. I had more energy, confidence, and clarity of mind. Still, I worried about what folks back home in both Oakland and Mexico would think. Cooking and eating are shared experiences, and so much

heart and pride go into breaking bread with others. The dishes of my childhood connected me to my family and my culture, as well as to El Barrio and the friends and neighbors who I considered part of la familia. If we couldn't share the same food, could we still sit down at the same table? Would we still have that sense of togetherness?

As it turns out, my family and culture are my greatest inspiration. I began to create vegan versions of generations-old recipes, without sacrificing the authentic Mexican flavors that my family expected and held dear. My relatives are as fiercely opinionated as they are passionate about food; it was a daunting challenge to give their time-honored recipes a plant-based makeover, even with las manos magicas. Getting their seal of approval is the highest compliment and means more to me than any award. The first vegan dish I made for them were my Jackfruit Tinga Tostadas (page 100). It's a dish that traditionally uses chicken, but the shredded jackfruit resembles meat so much that I didn't even tell my family members it was vegan. They absolutely loved it. My heart swelled with pride as, one by one, relatives told me how I'd nailed the sauce. It meant the world to me.

This book is about celebrating culture and family, cooking with compassion, and sharing meals with those we love most. I want to show you the Mexican and Latin flavors that we all love and crave, through a plant-focused lens. I invite you to join me in the kitchen and at the table. Provecho!

Tools and Pantry

Equip your kitchen with these items and you'll be set up for success. You may already be familiar with (or even have!) them, but I'll tell you why they're super-useful for vegan cooking.

TOOLS

You don't need a showroom's worth of fancy kitchen equipment to make plant-based recipes, but having these few essentials will make your life a lot easier.

Electric whisk

I use this tool often for whipping up aquafaba, which is the liquid from canned chickpeas and a miracle vegan alternative to egg whites. The electric whisk gets aquafaba as fluffy as meringue, without tiring out my wrist as a handheld whisk does.

High-powered blender

My Blendtec blender is my kitchen BFF. This powerful workhorse can make nut milks and fresh juices in a flash. It can also emulsify sauces and cremas, and has the blade action to break ingredients down into crumbs. A regular blender might not be strong enough to make things as creamy as they need to be; and because it has to work harder, the motor may heat up the contents, which isn't always desirable.

Multi-cooker

Like so many others, I'm obsessed with my Instant Pot. It can cook dried beans in minutes instead of hours. I use it to pressure-cook a vegan version of sancocho, and I can't replicate that flavor in a pot on the stove.

Silicone spatula

This is the heatproof cousin of the rubber spatula. I love using it to cook in cast-iron or nonstick skillets because it prevents them from getting scratched. The flexible head means I can get every last scrape of sauce from the pan.

PANTRY

These are the essential ingredients for cooking the recipes in this book. Some of them are incredible flavor boosters, while others lend a satisfying texture to dishes. For the uninitiated, I'll give you the low-down on some of my favorite items.

Latin Ingredients

These are my go-to spices and pantry staples for Latin cooking. Without them, I couldn't make most recipes—the food just wouldn't taste right. Except for the dried hibiscus and tamarind, which can be bought at Latin markets or general supermarkets in Latinx neighborhoods, you can find everything in a general supermarket.

All-purpose seasoning (salt-free): This seasoning blend has a little bit of black pepper, cumin, garlic powder, onion powder, bay leaf, oregano, and turmeric. Some varieties even have lemon powder and parsley. All-purpose seasoning is essential in my rice recipes, and in many traditional soups, stews, and empanadas. It's an easy way to get all the flavors you want without having to buy the individual spices.

Canned chipotle chiles in adobo: Chipotle chiles are dried red jalapeños (ripened all the way). When canned in adobo sauce, they're very smoky and add an amazing flavor to dishes besides bringing the heat. If you get them in a glass jar, they'll be spicier; the canned ones are generally less so. I like the reddish colored ones, which are milder and sweeter.

Cinnamon sticks: I prefer the Ceylon (aka canela) cinnamon that comes from trees in Sri Lanka. This thinner, brittle variety has a more vibrant flavor than cassia, which comes in thicker, harder sticks.

Dried hibiscus: Also called "jamaica" in Spanish, dried hibiscus makes a delicious tea. It has a tannic quality that adds complexity to agua fresca (see page 201) and countless cocktails. Look for dried hibiscus that's still intact—it will likely be fresher and deliver a stronger flavor. Depending on the flower, the color can range from very dark red to white.

Dried oregano: You would think that I use Mexican oregano in my Mexican cooking, but nope. I use "regular" oregano in the jar from the grocery store. It's very aromatic and strong. A little bit goes a long way. If there's cumin in a dish, there's probably oregano too. I use it often in soups and tacos.

Granulated garlic: I reach for this jar when I want to amp up the flavor of fresh garlic. Or I use it instead of fresh garlic when I want garlicky flavor without the spicy zing.

Ground cumin: Super-aromatic and earthy, this spice is excellent with meats but also equally wonderful with vegetables. It brings a musky aroma to food, which makes it taste more complex.

Ground turmeric: This is one of the ingredients in all-purpose seasoning; so if I don't use that in a dish, I usually add turmeric, along with cumin and oregano, to round out the flavors. It has a bitterness that's helpful in many ways. It can balance out sweetness, like in tomatoes. It can also compensate if you don't want to add salt. It even helps cut through the fat in rich dishes.

Hominy: Hominy is dried corn kernels that have been soaked in an alkali solution to soften the outer hulls. You can find purple or white hominy in cans. There's no real difference in flavor, so use them interchangeably. Hominy is pretty mild, which makes it an excellent vehicle for taking on flavor. Hominy's texture softens as it cooks in broth; it's a must in a rich pozole.

Paprika: Paprika was always one of those spices that seemed unnecessary. I never thought it had a strong enough flavor to make a difference. Well, I was wrong! When I omitted it from dishes, they didn't taste the way they should. Now I know it's a requirement for my braises and empanadas.

When you want smoky flavor but don't have the time to soak dried chiles, smoked paprika comes in handy. It's great for adding a bacon-y flavor to dishes. I use it a lot for taco fillings.

Tamarind: Mostly used for beverages in Mexico, tamarind is very savory, sweet, and, most of all, sour. Make sure the shells are still intact when you buy pods. If the shells are broken, the pulp inside can dry out.

Produce

A lot of Mexican and Latin food can be made with produce that's widely available everywhere; but here I've included some ingredients that may be harder to track down or that you might want to learn more about. Most of these can be found in large supermarkets nowadays or definitely in Latin markets.

Chiles: Many people associate fiery, fresh chiles with Mexican food, but it's the dried chiles that are the low-key stars of the cuisine. They're very traditional and form the backbone of so many soups, stews, and sauces. A lot of them look the same—wrinkly and brown, burgundy, or rusty red—but each one brings a different note to a dish. Dried chiles are especially helpful in plant-based cooking because they add deep, concentrated, smoky flavors to recipes. Most of the ones that I use can be found in general supermarkets.

- ÁRBOL—Chiles de árbol are small, narrow Mexican chiles that start out green, then mature to a bright red color before they're dried. At 15,000 to 30,000 on the Scoville scale (which measures "heat"), these small chiles pack a punch! They're similar in appearance and flavor to Japanese chiles or Italian peperoncino.

- CALIFORNIA—California chiles are the dried version of Anaheim chiles that have been allowed to mature to a red color and therefore have a slightly sweeter taste than the younger, green Anaheims. California chiles are very mild, just about 500 on the Scoville heat scale.

- **GUAJILLO**—Guajillos are one of the most popular Mexican chiles. They are actually the dried form of the mirasol chile. They are typically a dark reddish brown and have a slightly sweet flavor and a mild to moderate heat, clocking in at 2,500 to 5,000 Scoville heat units. They're used in a variety of sauces and broths, like in pozole rojo (see page 19), where they impart an orangey color.

- **JALAPEÑO**—These fresh chiles might be the friendliest. Don't worry about them being too spicy; there's heat, but it comes with great flavor.

- **PASILLA**—Pasillas are long and narrow chiles with a very dark brown or black color. Hence, the name, which translates to "little raisins." They are the dried form of the super-spicy chilaca chile, which starts out dark green and matures to a deep brown. Pasillas lend a rich, earthy, smoky flavor to sauces and dishes, and their heat varies greatly from a very mild 250 to a respectable 4,000 Scoville heat units.

- **POBLANO**—These fresh chiles are usually mild, but sometimes you get surprised with a little spice. I generally use green poblanos but sometimes you see red ones, which are sweeter. When shopping, choose flatter ones. The rounder poblanos are harder to char, and you'll most definitely need to char and peel them because the skin is too tough and leathery to eat. It's similar to how Italians char and peel red bell peppers.

- **SERRANO**—These fresh chiles are super-spicy. I typically use only one, or at most two, in a dish. Look for serranos with dried cracks on the body. That's a sign that they were picked at the right time.

Epazote: This herb is kind of like a combo of mint, basil, citrus, pine, oregano, and mustard greens. Yeah, it sounds weird, but that's epazote in a nutshell. It can be hard to find, so a good substitute is to use a little bit of fresh oregano, basil, and mint.

Mushrooms: Mushrooms have a meaty texture and savory flavor that make them a mainstay in vegan cooking. They also provide B12 vitamins, which prevent a type of anemia. I love fresh mushrooms in sauces and broths because they soak up flavors like a sponge. Most of the ones that I use (such as lion's mane, oyster, and shiitake) can be found at major supermarkets; but for some of the more exotic ones, check out your local farmers' markets or buy them from online mushroom farms.

- **CAULIFLOWER**—As the name suggests, this mushroom resembles a large bunch of cauliflower (or even egg noodles!). It has clusters of frills that range in color from white to yellow. Cauliflower mushrooms require a little longer cooking time than most other varieties, so they're perfect for simmering in soups. This may seem odd, but they're a great vegan substitute for tripe as they have a similar texture and appearance as well as an earthy, slightly nutty flavor. That's exactly how I use cauliflower mushrooms—as a stand-in for tripe in my menudo (see page 139).

- **LION'S MANE**—This fuzzy white mushroom looks like a big mop of fur, but those strands are actually the gills. The texture is soft, almost cottony, when raw. It then becomes juicy when cooked.

- **NEBRODINI BIANCO**—These fat, white mushrooms have the texture most similar to meat. As soon as you bite into one, juices flow out. Just thinking about them makes my mouth water. Nebrodini are very spongy and can soak up whatever flavor you throw at them.

- **OYSTER**—One of the most commonly cultivated mushrooms, these are widely available in grocery stores. You can easily recognize them by their silvery gray tops and white stems in natural cluster formations. They're sometimes called *pearl oyster mushrooms* or *tree oyster mushrooms*. They have a tender texture when cooked, and a subtle savory flavor. If you can't find some of the

more obscure types of mushrooms called for in my recipes, substitute oyster mushrooms.

- **SHIITAKE**—Shiitakes are tender, cream-colored mushrooms with brown caps. The stems can be tough, so feel free to remove them if you prefer a softer texture in your dishes. Their complex flavor is rich with umami—even more so when they're dried, which also gives them a subtle smokiness.

Nopales: These are prickly pear cactus pads. The flavor is slightly tangy and herbaceous, almost reminiscent of cucumber. You can find nopales at Latin markets, often already cooked and sliced, with the thorns shaved off. However, fresh nopales that are not pre-sliced will last longer in the fridge.

Plantains: Despite the similar appearance, plantains are *not* oversize bananas. They lean toward savory when unripe, and have a more caramelized texture after ripening. Green, unripe plantains are treated more like potatoes; they can be added to stews to thicken the broth. Yellow or dark plantains are the ripe ones and can become very sweet when cooked, like in maduros. Green plantains will take two weeks to turn yellow. To speed up the ripening, place them in a paper bag in a warm, dark place.

Yuca: This relative to cassava is kind of like an unsweetened sweet potato. Look beyond the fibrous texture and you have a tuber that lends amazing flavor to stews. They're also delicious when deep-fried, like french fries. Look for yuca with purple skin—it will often be covered in wax to keep it fresh. Choose the ones that are fatter; the skinny ones get dried out.

Vegan Ingredients

There was a time when you'd have to seek out vegan ingredients at a "health food" store; but plant-based diets have become so popular, you can find most everything at a big supermarket nowadays. Here are some tips for what to buy.

Aquafaba: Who knew that the liquid from canned chickpeas could whip up like egg whites? In this book, draining the liquid from a 29-ounce can should be enough for the recipes. For best results, buy high-quality canned chickpeas that are BPA-free, and make sure no salt is added.

Beans: Avoid dried beans that are shriveled up like raisins. That's a sign they're old and will take much longer to cook. Look for beans that are shiny and rounded. Pinto beans, in particular, will be more speckled when fresher. Beans are a great protein source, so make a big batch and serve them on the side when you need a protein boost.

When you don't have time to cook dried beans, the canned version is a good quick fix. Scan the contents list and make sure the cans are just packing beans and water—no salt. You can control the seasonings better that way.

Jackfruit, canned: This tropical fruit—grown in Southeast Asia, Africa, and Brazil—can be as big as your torso. There are two kinds that come in cans: yellow (sweet, ripe) jackfruit in syrup, and green (young, unripe). When you shred canned green jackfruit, it has the texture of pulled pork or chicken. I use green jackfruit packed in water as a filling for tacos and enchiladas. If the only kind of jackfruit you can find is canned in brine, give it a rinse before using.

Tofu: Almost all the tofu I use is pre-pressed (also called water-drained). You'll find it refrigerated in vacuum-sealed packages, usually in the dairy or produce aisle. It won't be packed in water, but it will be damp. Buying it pre-pressed saves you the trouble of draining and pressing it free of water when you get it home.

Vegan cheese: We're spoiled for choice with so many varieties of vegan cheese, but they're not all on the same level in terms of flavor or melting points. Look for products labeled "creamy" and made with ingredients such as coconut oil and soy. For quesadillas, I prefer slices rather than the pre-shredded stuff, which doesn't melt as well. "Sharp Cheddar" is usually a good one for quesadillas.

Vegan ground meat: I try to avoid calling out brand names, but there's one plant-based ground-meat substitute that's so far and above the rest. Impossible Meat has a great texture that resembles real meat so much that people who order Impossible Burgers think they've mistakenly been given beef instead.

Vegan sausage: Look for brands that don't have too many spices, as those may not play nicely with other ingredients. The sausages that I use have simple seasonings, such as onion, garlic, mushrooms, pepper, salt, and, maybe, paprika.

Vegetable broth: I generally use low-sodium vegetable broth when I want to control the amount of salt that goes into a dish. Other times, I like to use regular vegetable broth when I already know the dish requires more seasoning and will still need additional salt. Look for organic vegetable broth containing water, onion, celery, leeks, sea salt, citric acid, mushrooms, garlic, and spices. Some store-bought varieties contain tomato puree—just make sure it's a semi-clear vegetable broth for best results.

CHAPTER 1

La Mesa Llena

Mexican tables always have an abundance of food. La mesa llena, "the full table," is laden with several main dishes, plus salsa, tortillas, rice, beans, and other sides. It's a lot of food to prepare alone, which might be a reason why cooking is often a shared experience in Mexican culture.

In the neighborhood where I grew up, nobody had much money. But if we each brought something to the table, we ate like kings. I was raised by a single mother, though our family dinners were rarely just my mom, sister, and me. On many occasions, friends and neighbors would also join us, and family dinners turned into impromptu fiestas. There was one holiday weekend when more than fifty people showed up! We had so much food; we could've fed the entire barrio. Even as a kid, I knew this was something special.

Family dinners and celebrations didn't start when we sat down at the table. They started hours earlier in the kitchen, chopping onions or simmering a pot of stew. Cooking wasn't considered work that had to be done before the party started. Cooking *was* the party. The kitchen is my favorite place in the house to socialize and reconnect with family and friends. As we cook, we talk, sharing memories and recipes, both old and new.

In this chapter, the most traditional Mexican recipes are given a plant-based makeover of which even a Mexican abuelita would approve—and, luckily, mine does! These recipes are inspired by the dishes that filled the tables of my childhood—slow-simmered soups and stews, enchiladas, empanadas and tamales, and indispensable sides, like rice, beans, and tortillas.

La Mesa Llena is about celebrating culture and customs while creating new traditions and memories. It's about appreciating recipes that demand a little more time in the kitchen and encourage us to slow down and connect with those we love.

Pozole Rojo

Pozole is often served at birthday parties and special occasions but is also eaten as a hangover remedy. So it's good to have a big batch because you may need extra for the morning after!

I asked my aunts how to make the red version, and four couldn't tell me. The fifth could only list the ingredients without measurements. So, I had to reverse engineer this meatless version. I knew I had to create a smoky red broth that gets deep flavor and subtle heat from dried chiles. Instead of pork, I simmered mushrooms, which gave the dish a satisfying earthiness. My aunt said that my version looked like the real thing and she didn't miss the meat at all.

Even though it's meatless, you do need to let the broth simmer a while to allow the pozole to develop amazing flavor and soften the hominy.

MAKES 4 TO 6 SERVINGS

5 guajillo chiles

2 California chiles

3 tablespoons avocado oil

1 medium white or yellow onion, halved and thinly sliced

1½ pounds oyster mushrooms or lion's mane mushrooms, roughly chopped

3 dried bay leaves

3 garlic cloves

8 cups vegetable broth

5 cups canned hominy, rinsed and drained

1 teaspoon Himalayan pink salt

½ medium green cabbage, thinly shredded

8 to 10 radishes, sliced

4 limes, cut into wedges

2 cups chopped cilantro leaves and tender stems

Corn tortilla chips or corn tortillas (see page 44) for serving

Pop the stems off all the chiles and rip the chiles open a bit until you can shake out and discard the seeds. Transfer the chiles to a small saucepan and add just enough water to make the chiles float. Bring to a boil over high heat and boil for 8 minutes.

Meanwhile, in a large pot or Dutch oven over medium-high heat, warm the avocado oil. Add the onion, mushrooms, and bay leaves and cook, stirring occasionally, until the onion is transparent and the mushrooms are a little brown and crispy and just starting to release their liquid, about 8 minutes. Turn the heat to medium-low to prevent the mushroom liquid from cooking off because it will add delicious flavor to the broth. Watch them carefully!

Drain the chiles and place in a high-powered blender with the garlic and 4 cups of the vegetable broth. Blend until mostly smooth, about 30 seconds.

Strain the mixture through a fine-mesh sieve directly into the pot; discard the solids. Add the hominy, salt, and remaining 4 cups broth. If your pot isn't large enough to hold all the broth, reserve the excess and add it after the pozole reduces. Turn the heat to medium-high, cover the pot, and cook, undisturbed, until the hominy is well cooked, about 45 minutes. During the last 10 minutes of cooking, add any remaining broth (and up to 2 cups water if the liquid evaporated too quickly). Discard the bay leaves.

Let the pozole cool for 10 minutes, then serve with the cabbage, radishes, lime wedges, cilantro, and chips to add as desired.

Pozole Verde

◇

Whereas red pozole (see page 19) has a subtle heat, the green version is more intensely fiery from fresh chiles. We don't have a family recipe for green pozole, so I talked to my friend's mom to get inspiration for this version. She's from Oaxaca, where they add pepitas and sesame seeds to their pozole. The seeds give the broth a creaminess and a flavor that's reminiscent of tahini, while the fresh green chiles add a punch of heat.

**MAKES 4 TO
6 SERVINGS**

1 cup pepitas

⅓ cup sesame seeds

3 serrano chiles, stemmed

4 garlic cloves

½ large white onion, roughly chopped

1 bunch cilantro

2 cups water

4 cups canned hominy, rinsed and drained

Two 16-ounce packages pre-pressed tofu (see Note), cut into 1 by 2-inch slabs, or 32 ounces lion's mane mushrooms, roughly chopped

2 tablespoons white wine vinegar

2 teaspoons fine sea salt

6 cups vegetable broth

½ medium green cabbage, thinly shredded

8 to 10 radishes, sliced

3 to 4 limes, cut into wedges

Corn tortilla chips or corn tortillas (see page 44) for serving

Warm a large cast-iron skillet over medium heat for 2 to 3 minutes. Add the pepitas and sesame seeds and toast, stirring constantly, until browned, about 6 minutes for lightly browned, or 8 minutes for darker seeds with a more intense smoky flavor. (If the seeds begin to brown too quickly, turn the heat to medium-low.) Transfer to a high-powered blender and set aside.

Turn the heat to medium-high. Add the serranos and toast, turning occasionally, until lightly charred all over, 6 to 10 minutes. Add to the blender along with the garlic, onion, cilantro, and water and blend until smooth.

Strain the mixture through a fine-mesh sieve into a large stockpot; discard the solids. Add the hominy, tofu, vinegar, and salt and pour in the vegetable broth. If your pot isn't large enough to hold all the broth, reserve the excess and add it after the pozole reduces. Turn the heat to medium, cover the pot, and cook undisturbed until the hominy is well cooked, about 45 minutes. During the last 10 minutes of cooking, add any remaining broth (and up to 2 cups of water if the liquid evaporated too quickly).

Let the pozole cool for 10 minutes, then serve with the cabbage, radishes, lime wedges, and chips to add as desired.

NOTE Look for tofu in a vacuum-sealed package labeled "pre-pressed" or "water-drained." It won't be packed in water. If you can find only water-packed tofu, drain and place it between sheets of paper towels, then transfer everything to a plate. Top it with another plate, then weigh it down with a heavy can and set aside for 10 minutes to remove as much liquid as possible. Remove any excess water by squeezing the tofu in cheesecloth.

Pipian

◇

Pipian is a regional version of mole that's green. Instead of the earthier red mole, which is made with ancho and pasilla chiles, seeds, and chocolate, pipian is a brighter, fresher style made with poblanos and serranos.

My family always had pipian at parties, but it was usually some distant aunt or friend who made it. After much tinkering, I finally came up with this version, which is made with oyster mushrooms instead of chicken. Now, I'm the one who brings it to parties.

MAKES 6 TO 8 SERVINGS

Fine sea salt

2 tablespoons white vinegar

8 small russet potatoes, peeled and halved (or quartered, if large)

4 poblano chiles

2 to 4 serrano chiles (depending on heat preference)

1 cup dry-roasted assorted nuts (such as almonds, cashews, walnuts, pecans, hazelnuts; see Note)

¼ cup tightly packed cilantro leaves and tender stems, plus leaves for garnish

3 cups low-sodium vegetable broth

2 tablespoons avocado oil

8 ounces pink or white oyster mushrooms, roughly chopped

1 white onion, finely chopped

6 medium garlic cloves, minced

Spanish Rice (page 39) for serving

Bring 5 cups water to a boil over high heat. Add 1 teaspoon salt, 1 tablespoon of the vinegar, and the potatoes, then turn the heat to a simmer, cover, and continue to simmer for 15 minutes. Drain and set aside.

While the potatoes are simmering, place a poblano on a gas burner over medium-high heat. Char, turning occasionally with tongs, until 50 to 75 percent of the chile is charred, 4 to 6 minutes. Repeat with each poblano. Place the serranos on the burner and repeat the charring, about 2 minutes on each side. (If you don't have a gas burner, char them in a dry cast-iron skillet.) Set aside to cool.

In a high-powered blender, combine the nuts, ¼ cup cilantro, ¼ cup of the vegetable broth, the remaining 1 tablespoon vinegar, and ½ teaspoon salt. Set aside.

Peel most of the charred skin off the poblanos and serranos. You still want some charred bits to add a smoky flavor to the sauce. Slit each poblano on one side and remove and discard the seeds. Transfer all the chiles to the blender and blend on high speed until smooth, about 1 minute. Set this sauce aside.

In a large skillet or pot over medium heat, warm the avocado oil. Arrange the mushrooms in a single layer, working in batches if necessary to avoid overcrowding. Cook, undisturbed, until golden, about 3 minutes per side. They should be easy to flip once they are properly seared. Transfer to a bowl and set aside. Add the onion, garlic, and ¼ cup vegetable broth to the skillet. Cook, stirring occasionally, for 5 minutes. Add the sauce, mushrooms, potatoes, and remaining 2½ cups vegetable broth. Turn the heat to low, cover, and simmer until the sauce is thickened, about 15 minutes.

Serve the pipian over Spanish rice, garnished with cilantro leaves.

NOTE If you can't find packaged assorted nuts, use ¼ cup dry-roasted cashews, ¼ cup dry-roasted walnuts, and ½ cup dry-roasted almonds.

Sopa de Lentejas

This comforting lentil soup isn't something you'd see on a restaurant menu. It's very homey and, in fact, my mom made it often—probably because it's easy to prep. You pretty much just add all the ingredients to the pot and let it cook. (But make sure to soak the lentils in advance, for at least 2 hours.) There are many versions of sopa de lentejas, but something special that my mom adds is the cilantro at the end. That way, you get a bright, fragrant whiff as the residual heat opens up the flavors. Whenever I make this dish, it reminds me of mi mama.

MAKES 4 OR 5 SERVINGS

1 pound dried brown lentils, picked through and rinsed

2 tablespoons avocado oil

1 small or ½ large yellow onion, diced

1 serrano chile, diced

3 large garlic cloves, minced

2 large Roma tomatoes, diced

1 pound yellow potatoes, scrubbed and diced into ½-inch cubes

½ teaspoon dried parsley

2 teaspoons ground cumin

Fine sea salt

6 cups vegetable broth or water

¼ cup cilantro leaves and tender stems, roughly chopped

Cooked rice (see pages 39 to 43) for serving

Fermented Vegan Crema (page 163) for dolloping

Place the lentils in a large bowl, cover with water, and soak for at least 2 hours, or preferably overnight.

Warm a very large pot over high heat for 2 to 3 minutes, then turn the heat to medium. Add the avocado oil, onion, serrano, and garlic and cook, stirring occasionally, until the onion is translucent, about 5 minutes. Add the tomatoes and cook, stirring occasionally, until the tomatoes start to fall apart, release their juices, and tinge the other ingredients an appetizing orange color, 3 to 4 minutes.

Drain the lentils and transfer to the pot. Add the potatoes, parsley, cumin, and 2 teaspoons salt. Stir well, then add the vegetable broth. (If using water instead of broth, you may need to add more salt.) Turn the heat to high, bring to a simmer, and cover. Then turn the heat to low and let simmer until the lentils are cooked through, about 20 minutes if you soaked your lentils overnight; longer if you soaked them for only 2 hours. During the last 5 minutes of cooking, top with the cilantro.

Serve the sopa over rice, dolloped with crema.

Sopa de Fideo

—◇—

Tomato noodle soup is the kind of simple comfort food that all little kids love. In fact, I ate it every week growing up, and I still look to it when I want something that's easy on the stomach. The soup is usually made with chicken stock, but I use vegetable broth instead. I may be the only person to add crema to the dish. It's not traditional at all, but I love the creaminess. It gives the soup a richness that reminds me of curry.

MAKES 4 TO 6 SERVINGS

2 tablespoons avocado oil

7 ounces fideo (thin pasta)

2 large Roma tomatoes

¼ white or yellow onion, roughly chopped

1 garlic clove

1½ teaspoons fine sea salt

4 cups vegetable broth

2 cups water

2 carrots, peeled and cut into ¼ by 1-inch strips

Fermented Vegan Crema (page 163) for dolloping

Cilantro leaves for garnish (optional)

Warm a large pot over high heat for 2 to 3 minutes, then add the avocado oil and fideo. Turn the heat to medium-low and toast the fideo, stirring often, until the pasta is golden brown, about 8 minutes. Remove from the heat and set aside.

In a high-powered blender, combine the tomatoes, onion, garlic, salt, and 1 cup of the vegetable broth and blend until smooth. Pour into the pot with the fideo, add the water and remaining 3 cups vegetable broth, and set over medium heat. Cover partially and simmer for 10 minutes. Add the carrots and simmer, partially covered, until they're tender, about 15 minutes.

Serve the sopa dolloped with vegan crema and garnished with cilantro, if desired.

Mushroom Sancocho

Sancocho is a kind of braise with meat, root vegetables, and plenty of broth. Super-traditional throughout all of Latin America, the name comes from the verb *sancochar*, which means "to cook and let the juices release." And the juices sure do get released in this mushroom version!

I grew up eating the Salvadoran variation of sancocho, but the recipe here is based on the Colombian version. The dish is usually made in a pressure cooker to give the broth a better flavor and help the ingredients cook more quickly. Similarly, I like to make mine in an Instant Pot. It gives the mushrooms a meaty texture, and the flavors have nowhere to escape!

MAKES 6 TO 8 SERVINGS

3 tablespoons avocado oil

1 medium white onion, finely chopped

4 garlic cloves, minced

2 medium Roma tomatoes, chopped

1 cup finely chopped green onions

1 pound oyster mushrooms, roughly chopped

1 teaspoon ground cumin

1 teaspoon salt-free all-purpose seasoning

½ teaspoon paprika

¼ teaspoon ground turmeric

2 teaspoons fine sea salt

3 medium Yukon gold potatoes, scrubbed and roughly chopped

2 ears white corn, husked and quartered

1 medium yuca, peeled, halved lengthwise, and cut into ¾-inch-thick half-moons

1 green or slightly yellow plantain, peeled and cut into bite-size pieces

½ cup finely chopped cilantro leaves and tender stems, plus whole leaves for garnish

4 cups low-sodium vegetable broth

1 cup water

Lime wedges for serving (optional)

Set an Instant Pot or other multi-cooker to sauté on low (or set a large stockpot over medium-low heat). Add the avocado oil, white onion, and garlic and cook, stirring, until the onion is translucent and lightly browned, 4 to 5 minutes.

Add the tomatoes and green onions to the pot and cook, stirring occasionally, until the tomatoes release their liquid and soften up a little, 3 to 4 minutes. Add the mushrooms, cumin, all-purpose seasoning, paprika, turmeric, and salt and cook, stirring occasionally, until the mushrooms begin to release their liquid and the mixture begins to look stewy, 2 to 3 minutes. Add the potatoes, corn, yuca, plantain, chopped cilantro, vegetable broth, and water. Lock the lid, press the soup button, and pressure-cook for 12 minutes. (Or cover the pot and simmer over medium-low heat until the potatoes and yuca can be easily pierced with a fork, about 35 minutes.)

Ladle the sancocho into bowls, garnish with cilantro leaves, and serve with lime wedges.

Frijoles de la Olla

When it comes to beans, sometimes I want them refried; other times I want them whole, "beans in a cooking pot." If I'm having a stew, then a side of refried beans is too much mush on mush. But whole beans retain their texture, and I can even add them to the stew for a protein boost. Combine these beans with brown rice to form a complete protein.

MAKES 8 SERVINGS

3 cups dried pinto beans or black beans

10 to 12 cups water

½ white or yellow onion

3 garlic cloves

2 dried bay leaves

1 teaspoon fine sea salt

In a large bowl, cover the beans with 4 cups of the water and let soak for 10 to 12 hours.

Drain the beans and let them rest in a sieve for at least 2 hours (see Note).

Transfer the beans to a large pot. Add the onion, garlic, bay leaves, salt, and 6 cups water; bring to a boil over high heat. Cover partially and turn the heat to a simmer. Continue to simmer for 30 minutes, then check the amount of liquid in the pot. If most of it has evaporated, add the remaining 2 cups water and continue to simmer until the beans are soft (but not so mushy that they don't retain their shape) and the liquid in the pot has thickened, about 45 minutes. Discard the bay leaves.

Serve the beans hot.

NOTE Soaking the beans or any type of legume will help you digest them and prevent the, ahem, unwanted side effects that we associate with beans. Letting the beans drain for 2 hours activates the enzymes that aid digestion.

Instant Pot Frijoles Charros

———◇———

I really liked "cowboy beans" when I was growing up, even if back then I was removing the chunks of sausage and bacon. Now I make frijoles charros with shiitake mushrooms and vegan sausage.

It's funny to think of beans as celebratory, but this is a dish that's often served at parties. It's what people would start eating while waiting for the main courses to come out. It's a dish that's well suited for outdoor gatherings. I remember eating it out of cups in the fresh air, just like cowboys. An Instant Pot speeds up the cooking process, but you'll still need to soak the beans overnight before starting.

MAKES 8 TO 10 SERVINGS

3 tablespoons avocado oil

1 white onion, finely chopped

2 medium heirloom tomatoes, diced

5 garlic cloves, minced or pressed in a garlic press

1 jalapeño chile, finely chopped

1 serrano chile, finely chopped

½ pound shiitake mushrooms, sliced

4 vegan sausages, casings removed, sliced crosswise ½ inch thick

1 pound dried pinto beans, soaked in water overnight and drained

2 teaspoons ground cumin

2 teaspoons salt-free all-purpose seasoning

1½ tablespoons white wine vinegar

5 cups low-sodium vegetable broth

1 teaspoon fine sea salt

½ cup chopped cilantro leaves and tender stems

2 green onions, thinly sliced

Set an Instant Pot or other multi-cooker to sauté on low (or set a large stockpot over medium-low heat). Add the avocado oil and onion and cook, stirring, until the onion is translucent and slightly brown, about 4 minutes.

Add the tomatoes, garlic, jalapeño, and serrano to the pot and cook, stirring, until fragrant, 3 to 4 minutes. Add the mushrooms and vegan sausage and stir together. Add the beans, cumin, all-purpose seasoning, vinegar, vegetable broth, and salt. Lock the lid and set to pressure-cook on medium for 30 minutes. (Or cover the pot and bring to a boil over high heat, then turn the heat to medium, cover, and cook until the beans are tender and the broth has thickened but there's still a good amount of liquid, about 50 minutes.)

Serve the beans hot with a sprinkling of the cilantro and green onions.

Frijoles Rojos

These bright and bold-tasting beans are traditional in rural parts of Mexico. They're cooked with mild guajillo chiles, which color the dish red. You can have the beans as a side to rice dishes or eat the dish like a stew, which is how it's often consumed—as a protein-packed main to fill you up when you don't have meat.

MAKES 6 SERVINGS

4 guajillo chiles

1½ cups water

⅓ white or yellow onion

4 epazote leaves (optional)

1 teaspoon fine sea salt

2 tablespoons avocado oil

5 cups cooked pinto or black beans with their liquid (see page 31, onion removed) or canned beans

Vegan queso fresco (see page 164) for garnish

Chopped cilantro leaves and tender stems for garnish (optional)

Cooked rice (see pages 39 to 43) for serving (optional)

Pop the stems off the guajillos and rip the chiles open a bit until you can shake out and discard the seeds.

In a small saucepan combine the guajillos and water. Cover partially, set over high heat, and cook for 8 minutes. Pour the contents into a high-powered blender. Add the onion, epazote (if using), and salt and blend until smooth. Set aside.

Warm a large pot over medium heat for 2 to 3 minutes, add the avocado oil and the beans with their liquid, and then strain the pureed chiles through a sieve into the beans and stir well. Cover partially and boil until the liquid is reduced to a saucy consistency that coats the beans, about 15 minutes.

Serve the beans hot, garnished with vegan queso fresco and cilantro, with rice on the side, if desired.

Frijoles Colombianos

I learned to make this dish from my partner Gio's mom, who is Colombian. She says these beans are a staple in Colombia and "it's not a real party without them." It's kind of selling this dish short to just call it "beans." Yes, there are black beans, but also plenty of plantains, tomatoes, and potatoes. The dish is so hearty, I sometimes eat it as a meal in and of itself.

MAKES 4 TO 6 SERVINGS

2 tablespoons avocado oil

1 large white onion, cut into ½-inch cubes

2 small russet potatoes, cut into ½-inch cubes

2 small Roma tomatoes, cut into ½-inch cubes

1 large green or pale yellow plantain, cut into ½-inch cubes

1 cup vegetable broth

2 teaspoons ground cumin

2 teaspoons garlic powder

1 teaspoon smoked paprika

Two 15-ounce cans black beans; one drained and one undrained

Fine sea salt

Cilantro Rice (page 40) for serving

Guisado de Garbanzos (page 99) for serving

In a medium pot over medium heat, warm the avocado oil. Add the onion and cook, stirring, until the onion is translucent, about 3 minutes. Add the potatoes and cook, stirring occasionally, for 4 minutes. Add the tomatoes, plantain, vegetable broth, cumin, garlic powder, paprika, all the beans plus the liquid, and 1 teaspoon salt. Cover the pot and bring to a simmer, then turn the heat to medium-low and cook until the dish is saucy and stewy, about 20 minutes. Taste and season with salt, as needed.

Serve the beans hot with cilantro rice and chickpea guisado.

Spanish Rice

Pair this rice with refried pinto beans (see page 103) and serve with any main course. Some of my favorites are chilaquiles (see pages 125 and 126), Chiles Rellenos (page 85), and Guisado de Garbanzos (page 99).

MAKES 4 TO 6 SERVINGS

1½ cups white jasmine rice

3 tablespoons avocado oil

3 Roma tomatoes, halved

¼ large white onion, halved

3 garlic cloves, halved

2½ cups low-sodium vegetable broth

1 tablespoon salt-free all-purpose seasoning

1 teaspoon fine sea salt

Thoroughly rinse the rice in a fine-mesh sieve under running water until the water is clear. Drain in the sieve for 10 minutes.

In a large pot over medium heat, warm the avocado oil. Add the rice and cook, stirring often, until golden brown, 6 to 8 minutes.

In a high-powered blender, combine the tomatoes, onion, garlic, and 1 cup of the vegetable broth and blend until smooth.

Pour the mixture into the rice; add the all-purpose seasoning, salt, and remaining 1½ cups vegetable broth; and stir together. Bring to a boil, then turn the heat to low. Cover and cook for 12 minutes.

Remove from the heat and keep covered for 10 minutes before serving.

Cilantro Rice

Someone asked me, "How do I know what kind of rice to serve with a dish?" There's no hard-and-fast rule; but if the dish is orange, I generally recommend serving it with green rice, like this cilantro-flecked option. It's more colorful and the flavors will complement each other without repeating the same notes.

MAKES 4 TO 6 SERVINGS

1½ cups white jasmine rice (see Note)

2 tablespoons avocado oil

½ yellow onion, roughly chopped

2 large garlic cloves

2 cups lightly packed roughly chopped cilantro leaves, plus more for garnish (optional)

3 cups low-sodium vegetable broth

½ teaspoon fine sea salt

Thoroughly rinse the rice in a fine-mesh sieve under running water until the water is clear. Drain in the sieve for 10 minutes.

In a large pot over medium heat, warm the avocado oil. Add the rice and cook, stirring often, until golden brown, about 6 minutes.

In a high-powered blender, combine the onion, garlic, 2 cups cilantro, 2 cups of the vegetable broth, and the salt and blend until smooth.

Pour the mixture into the rice. Swirl the remaining 1 cup vegetable broth in the blender to release any stuck bits, then pour into the pot. Bring the rice to a simmer, cover, and turn the heat to medium-low. Cook for 15 minutes at a simmer, turning the heat to low if the rice starts to boil.

Remove from the heat and keep covered for 10 minutes before serving. Garnish with cilantro, if desired.

NOTE If using brown jasmine rice, increase the amount of vegetable broth to 4 cups. Blend 3 cups with the vegetables, then rinse the blender with the remaining 1 cup.

Arroz Amarillo

Of the various rices, "yellow rice" is my favorite to eat by itself. Typically, it's served with pozole, chile verde, sopa de lentejas—any dish that has some broth so you can mix it with the rice. The traditional version is made with chicken broth or a bouillon cube. I use vegetable broth instead to fortify the rice with flavor.

MAKES 6 SERVINGS

1½ cups long-grain white rice

1 pinch saffron

½ cup hot water

2 tablespoons avocado oil

½ yellow or white onion, quartered

2 large Roma tomatoes, halved

3 garlic cloves

2 cups low-sodium vegetable broth

1 tablespoon salt-free all-purpose seasoning

1 teaspoon fine sea salt

2 cups frozen mixed vegetables (such as carrots, peas, and corn)

Thoroughly rinse the rice in a fine-mesh sieve under running water until the water is clear. Drain in the sieve for 10 minutes. Combine the saffron with the hot water and let soak for up to 10 minutes.

In a large pot over medium heat, warm the avocado oil. Add the rice and cook, stirring often, until golden brown, 6 to 8 minutes.

In a high-powered blender, combine the onion, tomatoes, garlic, and 1 cup of the vegetable broth and blend until smooth.

Pour the mixture into the rice; add the saffron and soaking liquid, all-purpose seasoning, salt, and remaining 1 cup vegetable broth; and stir together. Turn the heat to high and bring to a simmer. Stir in the frozen vegetables, cover, turn the heat to medium-low, and simmer for 15 minutes.

Remove from the heat and keep covered for 10 minutes before serving.

Corn Tortillas

Traditional corn tortillas are 100 percent masa. I cut my masa with some all-purpose flour, an import that came to Mexico with the Spaniards. My aunt makes her tortillas this way, and I love how they are fluffier and puff up with an air pocket, almost like pita. They also last longer, whereas all-corn tortillas become too hard very quickly. These tortillas also reheat better.

MAKES
10 TORTILLAS

2 cups instant corn or blue corn masa flour (such as Maseca)

1 cup all-purpose flour

1½ cups warm water, plus 2 tablespoons

2 teaspoons fresh lime juice

Fine sea salt

Avocado oil for frying

In a large bowl, combine the masa and all-purpose flour. Add the 1½ cups water, ¼ cup at a time, mixing it in with your hands until a stiff but flexible dough forms. Add the lime juice and a hefty pinch of salt and mix well but do not overwork the dough. It should be moist, with no cracks when you flatten it. If it gets cracks, knead in the remaining water, 1 tablespoon at a time, until the dough is ready.

Pinch the dough into ten equal mounds and roll each one between your palms to form a ball. (The dough will dry out if left unattended. Rinse your hands with water to knead moisture back into the dough.)

Next, get out a tortilla press; or if you don't have one, use two large hardcover books. Cut a clean compostable bag (the thin, plastic-like kind) into a 20 by 10-inch rectangle. Make sure there are no holes in it. Place half of the rectangle over the bottom plate of the tortilla press (or on the bottom book) and place a dough ball in the center.

Fold the other half of the rectangle over the dough, so it's neatly in half with the dough ball centered in between the two layers. If using a tortilla press, slowly close the press to form the tortilla. If using books, firmly press down with the top book to form a 5- to 6-inch tortilla. You should be able to peel the tortilla off in one piece and set it aside. Repeat with the remaining balls of dough.

Warm a large skillet, preferably cast-iron, over high heat for 4 to 5 minutes, then turn the heat to medium-low and add a dash of avocado oil, swirling it evenly over the bottom. Cook one or two tortillas at a time in a single layer. (A 12-inch skillet can fit two tortillas at once.) If making tortillas to reheat and serve later, cook for 45 seconds on each side. If serving right away, cook for 1 minute 15 seconds on each side. If needed, add more oil to cook more tortillas.

Store the tortillas in a resealable plastic bag or airtight glass container for up to 3 days.

Flour Tortillas

I hope I'm not bursting any bubbles by telling you that traditional, handmade flour tortillas have lard. That's what gives them that melt-in-your-mouth flakiness. Well, that and the labor of shaping them by hand so they're thin enough. According to my grandma, if your flour tortilla isn't thin enough, it's just pita bread. And you definitely want the tortillas to be thin when you use them for burritos and quesadillas.

I substitute avocado oil for the lard to mimic that softness, and the resulting flavor is milder—I actually enjoy it more than the fatty porkiness of lard. This recipe has just a few ingredients, but the technique requires some practice. It involves slapping the dough and throwing it around to stretch out the gluten, like a mini pizza. My grandma taught me to make these tortillas over FaceTime. She can make each tortilla in 30 seconds. It takes me 3 minutes. Like I said, it takes practice, and she's been practicing all her life. I hope I get to her level one day.

MAKES 6 TO 8 SMALL TORTILLAS, OR 4 OR 5 LARGE TORTILLAS

2 cups all-purpose flour, plus more for sprinkling

3 tablespoons avocado oil

1 cup warm water

1 teaspoon fine sea salt

In a large bowl, combine the flour and avocado oil and mix with your hands until it becomes crumbly. In a liquid measuring cup, stir together the warm water and salt and then add it slowly to the bowl. Keep mixing the dough with your hands until thoroughly combined—it should be moist and sticky but still crumbly.

Dump the dough onto a floured work surface. Knead the dough, sprinkling with flour, until silky smooth, 10 to 12 minutes. (If you want to make the dough in advance, wrap it in plastic wrap and refrigerate for up to 7 days.) Using your hands, roll the dough into a log and then use a bench scraper or a knife to slice into six to eight, or four or five, even pieces. Working with one piece at a time, roll into a ball between your hands. Set aside.

Warm a large skillet, preferably cast-iron, over high heat for 4 to 5 minutes, then turn the heat to medium-low. Now comes the tricky part—you have to stretch and flatten the tortillas by hand. This technique takes some getting used to, but you will improve with practice.

CONTINUED

Flour your hands and begin slapping the dough ball back and forth between your open, flat palms. You want to smash it a bit when you slap your hands together, but you also want to gain momentum with your swing. As the ball flattens and the round of dough grows in diameter, the edges will begin to hang over the edges of your hands. This is essential to flatten the dough, as gravity and the momentum of your swing will help pull and stretch the dough. Be sure to rotate the round as you slap to make an even, round tortilla. When you're done, the dough should be thin enough to be nearly transparent.

Place the flattened tortilla directly on the dry skillet and cook for 3 minutes on each side. (As that tortilla cooks, you can begin flattening the next one.)

Serve the tortillas warm.

NOTE If you're making the tortillas in advance, I suggest cooking them for 1 minute on each side; it's better to undercook so when you reheat them, they're soft and not stiff. Store in a resealable plastic bag in the refrigerator for up to 3 days.

VARIATION

If you really can't get the hang of hand-forming your tortilla, don't fret! It is possible to roll them out flat, but they *won't* come out as thin as the hand-pressed tortillas. The texture will be different, but still amazing. If you decide to roll your tortillas, cut the dough log into about ten smaller pieces. This will leave you enough room on your work surface to roll them as thin as possible. Cook as directed.

No-Bake Enchiladas Verde with Jackfruit

You can make these enchiladas completely on the stove top. They're coated with a salsa verde that's bright and tangy from tomatillos. If you want to smother them with cheese, arrange the enchiladas in a baking dish, sprinkle with a good melting vegan cheese, then pop them in the oven for a few minutes.

MAKES 16 TO 20 ENCHILADAS

TOMATILLO SALSA

7 medium tomatillos, husked

1 Roma tomato

3 jalapeño chiles (remove the seeds if you want less heat)

½ large white onion, quartered

3 garlic cloves

¾ cup packed finely chopped cilantro leaves and tender stems

1½ cups low-sodium vegetable broth

1 tablespoon ground cumin

½ teaspoon fine sea salt

5 to 6 tablespoons avocado oil

Two 20-ounce cans young (green) jackfruit in water, drained

16 to 20 corn tortillas (see page 44)

3 cups thinly shredded green cabbage

"Sour cream" (vegan cream cheese mixed with water) or Vegan Chipotle Crema (page 160) for topping

Vegan queso fresco (see page 164) for topping

To make the salsa: Set a large cast-iron skillet over medium-high heat. Place the tomatillos, tomato, jalapeños, and onion in the dry skillet and cook, turning a few times, until lightly charred all over, 6 to 8 minutes. As each ingredient is charred, transfer to a high-powered blender, then add the garlic and cilantro and blend until smooth.

Pour the tomatillo mixture into a large stainless-steel skillet and add the vegetable broth, cumin, and salt. Set over high heat, stir well, and bring to a simmer. Turn the heat to low and simmer, partially covered, until thickened, 10 to 12 minutes. Remove from the heat and set aside.

Meanwhile, set a large nonstick skillet over medium heat and add 1 tablespoon of the avocado oil. Shred the jackfruit into the hot skillet and cook, stirring occasionally, until crispy, about 10 minutes. By this time, the salsa should be ready. Add 1 cup of the salsa to the jackfruit, turn the heat to medium-low, and simmer for 5 minutes. Remove from the heat and set aside.

Set another cast-iron skillet (or clean the one used to char the vegetables) over medium heat and add 1 tablespoon avocado oil. Prepare an assembly line by toasting each tortilla in the skillet, about 15 seconds per side; add 1 tablespoon avocado oil after toasting every four tortillas. Then, dip a toasted tortilla in the salsa and lay on a plate. Add a spoonful of the jackfruit filling and roll into a cylinder. Repeat with the remaining tortillas and jackfruit, dividing among four plates.

Top the enchiladas with the cabbage, "sour cream," and vegan queso fresco and serve.

Colombian Empanadas

Mexican empanadas are usually sweet (see Sweet Potato Empanadas, page 235, and Apple Empanadas, page 238). Colombia and other South American countries make savory empanadas. I had never tried a savory empanada until I was at my Colombian friend's house as a kid and her mom said we were having empanadas for dinner. I was so excited because I thought I was having dessert for dinner.

However, I wasn't disappointed by her mom's empanadas, by any means. The filling was potato and beef in a crisp crust made from masa. I remember they were so simple and satisfying. Traditionally, empanadas are fried; but nowadays, they're often baked to avoid all the oil. I omit the beef and double up on the potatoes for my version. They're all so good with aji, a salsa-like condiment that reminds me of tabouli.

MAKES 20 TO 24 EMPANADAS

BASIC EMPANADA DOUGH

2 pinches saffron

1 cup warm (not hot!) water, plus 2 cups room-temperature water

4 cups instant corn masa flour (such as Maseca), plus more for dusting

1½ tablespoons salt-free all-purpose seasoning

2 teaspoons fine sea salt

1 tablespoon avocado oil

FILLING

2 tablespoons avocado oil

½ large yellow onion, finely chopped

4 large garlic cloves, minced or pressed with a garlic press

4 medium Yukon gold potatoes, scrubbed and diced

2 Roma tomatoes, diced

¼ cup finely chopped cilantro leaves and tender stems

1 tablespoon white wine vinegar

1 teaspoon ground cumin

1 teaspoon paprika

⅛ teaspoon dried sage

1 teaspoon Himalayan pink salt

2 tablespoons vegetable broth

Coconut oil for frying

Aji (page 156) for dipping

To make the dough: In a liquid measuring cup, combine the saffron with the warm water and let soak until the water becomes dark yellow, 15 to 20 minutes.

In a large bowl, combine the masa, all-purpose seasoning, and sea salt and whisk well. Set aside.

Strain the saffron water through a fine-mesh sieve into the room-temperature water, then slowly pour that into the masa mixture, mixing with your hands or a wooden spoon until all the water has been incorporated. Add the avocado oil and mix with your hands until the dough forms a ball, then cover and set aside.

CONTINUED

To make the filling: Warm a large skillet over high heat for 4 to 5 minutes. Turn the heat to medium; add the avocado oil, onion, and garlic; and cook, stirring often, until the onion is translucent and slightly brown, about 4 minutes. Add the potatoes and cook, stirring occasionally, for 3 minutes. Add the tomatoes, cilantro, vinegar, spices, and pink salt and cook, stirring and scraping the browned bits from the bottom of the skillet with a wooden spoon, until the tomatoes release their juices. Add the vegetable broth and stir. Cover and simmer, stirring every 3 to 4 minutes to prevent serious sticking (it will stick a little) until the potatoes are tender, about 15 minutes. Remove from the heat and let cool.

Dust your work surface with masa. Dump your dough ball onto it and cut into four pieces. The dough should feel moist and supple; if it feels too dry, sprinkle with some water. (The dryness of the masa depends on how old it is, so use your best judgment to achieve a dough that's easy to roll and not too sticky.)

Dust your hands and a rolling pin with masa and roll the dough, one piece at a time, to about ¼ inch thick. Using a 4-inch cookie cutter or cup, stamp out rounds from the dough. Reroll the scraps, sprinkling with water if needed, to stamp out more rounds.

Add about 1 tablespoon of the filling to the center of each round of dough; wet your hands and dab the edges with water. Fold each empanada into a half-moon and use your damp hands to pinch and seal the edges shut. If the empanada sticks to the work surface, gently pry it off with a spatula. Rinse your hands before forming each new empanada to make sure they're sufficiently damp.

Line a baking sheet with several layers of paper towels.

Warm a large skillet over medium heat for 2 to 3 minutes, then turn the heat to medium-low and add about 1 cup coconut oil (or enough to fry the empanadas); warm until bubbles form around a wooden chopstick when inserted in the oil. Working in batches, carefully add a few empanadas and fry until the bottoms are golden and the tops puff up a little, about 4 minutes. If the empanadas brown too quickly, lower the heat. Flip and fry until the other side is golden, about 3 minutes. Remove to the prepared baking sheet.

Enjoy the empanadas with some aji for dipping.

Lentil-Cauliflower Empanadas

◇

I'm happiest when I'm cooking alongside my family and friends. When I couldn't see my mom in person, she and I created this recipe over FaceTime. It made me happy that she was learning about plant-based cooking; changing her perspective on how an "authentic" dish doesn't need meat. She also appreciated these empanada were still stuffed with nourishing ingredients.

MAKES 20 TO 24 EMPANADAS

FILLING

8 ounces dried brown lentils, picked through and rinsed

2 tablespoons avocado oil

½ large yellow onion, finely chopped

4 garlic cloves, minced or pressed with a garlic press

1 teaspoon dried oregano

1 teaspoon ground cumin

½ teaspoon ground turmeric

1 tiny pinch ground nutmeg

1 teaspoon Himalayan pink salt

2 pinches freshly ground black pepper

½ large head cauliflower, finely chopped

Instant corn masa flour (such as Maseca) for dusting

Basic Empanada Dough (see page 52)

Coconut oil for frying

Aji (page 156) for dipping

To make the filling: In a large bowl, cover the lentils with water and let soak for at least 4 hours, or preferably overnight.

Warm a large skillet over high heat for 4 to 5 minutes. Turn the heat to medium, add the avocado oil and onion, and cook, stirring often, until translucent and browned, about 4 minutes. Add the garlic, oregano, cumin, turmeric, nutmeg, salt, and pepper and cook, stirring, until fragrant, about 2 minutes. Add the cauliflower and cook, stirring, for 3 minutes more. Add 4 cups water, cover, and simmer until the cauliflower is tender, about 30 minutes. Remove from the heat and let cool.

Dust your work surface with masa. Dump your dough ball onto it and cut into four pieces. The dough should feel moist and supple; if it feels too dry, sprinkle with some water. (The dryness of the masa depends on how old it is, so use your best judgment to achieve a dough that's easy to roll and not too sticky.)

Dust your hands and rolling pin with masa and roll the dough, one piece at a time, to about ¼ inch thick. Using a 4-inch cookie cutter or cup, stamp out rounds from the dough. Reroll the scraps, sprinkling with water if needed, to stamp out more rounds.

Add about 1 tablespoon of the filling to the center of each round of dough; wet your hands and dab the edges with water. Fold each empanada into a half-moon and use your damp hands to pinch and seal the edges shut. If the empanada sticks to the work surface, gently pry it off with a spatula. Rinse your hands before forming each new empanada to make sure they're sufficiently damp.

Line a baking sheet with several layers of paper towels.

Warm a large skillet over medium heat for 2 to 3 minutes, then turn the heat to medium-low and add about 1 cup coconut oil (or enough to fry the empanadas); warm until bubbles form around a wooden chopstick when inserted in the oil. Working in batches, carefully add a few empanadas and fry until the bottoms are golden and the tops puff up a little, about 4 minutes. If the empanadas brown too quickly, lower the heat. Flip and fry until the other side is golden, about 3 minutes. Remove to the prepared baking sheet.

Enjoy the empanadas with some aji for dipping.

Mushroom-Spinach Empanadas

I remember having a spinach empanada while roaming San Francisco. I loved how simple and creamy it was, so I had to try to re-create it. I added mushrooms to my version to bump up the earthy flavor and give the filling a great texture.

MAKES 20 TO 24 EMPANADAS

FILLING

2 tablespoons avocado oil

½ large yellow onion, finely chopped

4 garlic cloves, minced or pressed with a garlic press

1 pound white mushrooms, quartered

1 teaspoon Himalayan pink salt

3 handfuls spinach

8 ounces shredded vegan cheese

Instant corn masa flour (such as Maseca) for dusting

Basic Empanada Dough (see page 52)

Coconut oil for frying

Aji (page 156) for dipping

To make the filling: Set a large skillet over medium-high heat, then add the avocado oil. Add the onion and garlic and cook, stirring often, until the onion is slightly translucent and brown, about 4 minutes. Add the mushrooms and salt and cook, stirring occasionally, until the mushrooms have released most of their liquid, about 6 minutes. Continue cooking, stirring occasionally, until the liquid has cooked off, about 2 minutes. Add the spinach and cook, stirring, until wilted, about 2 minutes more. Remove from the heat and let cool, then stir in the vegan cheese.

Dust your work surface with masa. Dump your dough ball onto it and cut into four pieces. The dough should feel moist and supple; if it feels too dry, sprinkle with some water. (The dryness of the masa depends on how old it is, so use your best judgment to achieve a dough that's easy to roll and not too sticky.)

Dust your hands and rolling pin with masa and roll the dough, one piece at a time, to about ¼ inch thick. Using a 4-inch cookie cutter or cup, stamp out rounds from the dough. Reroll the scraps, sprinkling with water if needed, to stamp out more rounds.

Add about 1 tablespoon of the filling to the center of each round of dough; wet your hands and dab the edges with water. Fold each empanada into a half-moon and use your damp hands to pinch and seal the edges shut. If the empanada sticks to the work surface, gently pry it off with a spatula. Rinse your hands before forming each new empanada to make sure they're sufficiently damp.

Line a baking sheet with several layers of paper towels.

Warm a large skillet over medium heat for 3 to 4 minutes, then turn the heat to medium-low and add about 1 cup coconut oil (or enough to fry the empanadas); warm until bubbles form around a wooden chopstick when inserted in the oil. Working in batches, carefully add a few empanadas and fry until the bottoms are golden and the tops puff up a little, about 4 minutes. If the empanadas brown too quickly, lower the heat. Flip and fry until the other side is golden, about 3 minutes. Remove to the prepared baking sheet.

Enjoy the empanadas with some aji for dipping.

Ama's Tacos Ricos

My mom created these delicious lettuce tacos specifically for me because I'm plant-based. She uses the same technique as for preparing carne asada: cook the vegan meat substitute 'til crispy, then push it to one side of the pan and add the vegetables. Doing this incorporates the juices from the vegan meat into the onions and creates a flavor bomb of umami. Do *not* overmix the onions with the meat or the meat won't get crispy. She wraps the filling in crunchy lettuce leaves instead of tortillas because she likes the hot and cold contrast.

MAKES 8 TO 10 LETTUCE TACOS

3 tablespoons avocado oil

One 12-ounce package vegan ground-meat substitute

¾ teaspoon paprika

¾ teaspoon ground cumin

½ teaspoon granulated garlic (see Note)

1 teaspoon fine sea salt

1 medium white or yellow onion, sliced into ½ by 3-inch strips

2 garlic cloves, minced

2 large poblano chiles, preferably one red and one green, sliced into ½ by 3-inch strips

1 cup frozen green peas, thawed

8 to 10 large romaine lettuce leaves

Avocado Salsa (page 155) for serving

Lime wedges for squeezing

Warm a large stainless-steel skillet over medium heat for 2 to 3 minutes. Add 2 tablespoons of the avocado oil and swirl to coat the bottom of the skillet. Add the vegan ground meat and cook, stirring, until browned and starting to crisp, 4 to 5 minutes. Add the paprika, cumin, granulated garlic, and salt and cook for 2 minutes more, stirring until the spices are well combined and the meat is crispy. Move all the meat to one side of the skillet and add the remaining 1 tablespoon avocado oil. Add the onion and minced garlic and cook, stirring often, until the onion is slightly trans-lucent, 4 to 5 minutes. Stir the onion together with the meat.

Add the poblanos and peas to the skillet, stir to combine, and cook until the mixture is caramelized and fragrant. Remove from the heat and let sit, partially covered, to cool a bit.

Add a generous portion of the filling to each lettuce leaf, top with avocado salsa and a squeeze of lime, and serve immediately.

NOTE The difference between granulated garlic and garlic powder isn't so straightforward. A lot of brands are labeled "garlic powder" but actually have a fine-salt texture, like granulated garlic. I prefer to use granulated garlic; but if what you have is more powdery, just use a little less than the amount called for.

CHAPTER 2

La Mesita

When I left for college, I felt lonely without my family and friends from back home. Cooking became a way to meet people and form a new community. No one I knew in college was cooking anything that resembled a family dinner, so I took up that mantle and started inviting people over. We'd gather around my kitchen mesita, "small table," to share simple, casual meals.

As I ventured into plant-based cooking, I was grateful to have a hungry audience eager to try my new recipes. I fed my friends familiar dishes such as tacos, quesadillas, and taquitos, loaded up with vegetables instead of the usual meat and cheese, and all the intense flavors that satisfy a hankering for Mexican food.

When I crave Mexican food, I want the smoky, fruity flavors from fresh and dried chiles. I desire fresh oregano and marjoram as well as dried bay leaf and cloves. I look for garlic and onions, which are the foundation of almost every Mexican dish. I long for creamy avocado, crunchy pickled vegetables, and spicy salsa—all on one plate.

In my vegan recipes, I like to play around with ingredients that aren't traditionally Mexican—such as jackfruit and shiitake mushrooms—but I often also include produce that's commonly found in Mexican cuisine, like tomatoes, corn, zucchini, squash, chiles, and potatoes.

The dishes in this chapter are inspired by the first meals that I cooked for friends when I was newly vegan. These recipes show how easy vegan cooking can be. Delicious vegan food doesn't have to be fussy!

La Mesita re-creates the feelings of kinship and camaraderie that I missed from home, just on a smaller scale. It is a celebration of both the culture in which I grew up and the power of vegan food to create new traditions and bring together new friends.

Adobo Mushroom Tacos

A funny thing, Latinos use an adobo seasoning mix and that's all my mom knew about it. She likes the flavors that come with the spices in the seasoning. Now, I make my own adobo spice blend for my famous adobo mushroom tacos. They're the most requested dish at family gatherings and potlucks with friends.

Roasted chanterelle mushrooms are especially good in these tacos because they have a chewy texture that satisfies, like a meat filling. I add a sprinkle of coconut sugar and cayenne pepper, which give the chanterelles an addictive sweet-spicy flavor.

As good as the tacos are, don't even think about skipping any of the toppings! Fill each tortilla with mushrooms, salsa, crema, and cilantro for an unbelievable combo of flavors and textures in every bite. Everyone should have such a trusty recipe in their back pocket to bring to gatherings. Try it and these could become *your* famous adobo tacos too!

MAKES 8 TO 10 SERVINGS

5 cups roughly chopped fresh chanterelle mushrooms

¼ cup finely chopped white onion, or 1 tablespoon granulated onion

2 tablespoons fresh lime juice

2 tablespoons avocado oil

1 tablespoon dried oregano

2 teaspoons ground cumin

2 teaspoons garlic powder

2 teaspoons coconut sugar

1 teaspoon fine sea salt

¼ to ½ teaspoon cayenne pepper (depending on heat preference)

Corn tortillas (see page 44) for serving

Salsa (see pages 147 to 156) for serving

Vegan crema (see pages 159 to 163) for serving

Halved cherry tomatoes for serving (optional)

Sliced radishes for serving (optional)

Chopped cilantro leaves and tender stems for serving

Lime wedges for squeezing

Preheat the oven to 400°F.

In a medium bowl, combine the mushrooms, onion, lime juice, avocado oil, oregano, cumin, garlic powder, coconut sugar, salt, and cayenne and stir together. Spread the mushrooms in a single layer on a rimmed baking sheet.

Roast the mushrooms until they reach your desired texture—I like them golden brown, about 20 minutes. The longer the mushrooms roast, the crispier and drier they will be.

Warm a medium skillet over medium heat for 3 to 4 minutes. Add each tortilla and warm until it is pliable, 15 to 25 seconds per side.

Fill the tortillas with the mushrooms; add some salsa, vegan crema, tomatoes and radishes (if desired), and cilantro; squeeze on some lime juice; and serve immediately.

Shredded Jackfruit Tacos

Canned jackfruit (the green kind, not the sweet one packed in syrup) has become popular with plant-based eaters because, when pulled apart, it mimics the texture of shredded meat. For the filling here, the key is to cook the jackfruit with oil so it becomes crispy but falls apart. Then simmer it in the sauce to saturate it with amazing flavors. (Just cooking in the sauce without crisping makes it gummy.) The sauce is semi-traditional Yucatan style, inspired by adobo and al pastor. It's smoky, and tart from the fresh orange juice.

MAKES 8 TACOS

5 tablespoons avocado oil

½ white onion, finely chopped

5 garlic cloves, minced

6 guajillo chiles

1 teaspoon cumin seeds

⅓ cup fresh orange juice

¾ cup low-sodium vegetable broth

1 large tomato, roughly chopped

1 tablespoon dried oregano

1 tablespoon paprika or smoked paprika

1 teaspoon fine sea salt

Two 20-ounce cans young (green) jackfruit in water, rinsed and drained

8 corn tortillas (see page 44) or flour tortillas (see page 47), warmed

Pico de Gallo (page 147) for topping

Vegan Cilantro Crema (page 159) for topping

Sliced avocado for topping (optional)

Finely chopped cilantro leaves and tender stems for topping

Lime wedges for squeezing

In a large skillet over medium heat, warm 2 tablespoons of the avocado oil. Add the onion, garlic, guajillos, and cumin seeds and cook, stirring, until the oil takes on a bit of color from the guajillos and cumin, about 4 minutes. (Lower the heat if anything browns too quickly.) Turn the heat to low and cook, stirring, until the guajillos are reddish brown, not burnt or dark brown, about 2 minutes. Remove the guajillos and set aside. Transfer the onion mixture to a high-powered blender.

Stem and seed the guajillos, then add to the blender. Add the orange juice, vegetable broth, tomato, oregano, paprika, and salt and blend until smooth. Set this sauce aside.

Shred the jackfruit with your hands until it looks like shredded chicken. Pat dry with paper towels and set aside.

Warm a large stainless-steel or nonstick skillet over medium heat for 4 to 5 minutes, then add the remaining 3 tablespoons avocado oil and let get hot. Add the jackfruit and cook, stirring occasionally, until it is golden brown and crispy, about 8 minutes. Lower the heat and cook until the jackfruit is browned, about 5 minutes more, stirring in 1 tablespoon water if the jackfruit starts to stick to the skillet. Turn the heat to medium-high, strain the sauce into the skillet, and bring to a boil. Turn the heat to medium, cover partially, and let simmer until the sauce has thickened and most of the liquid has evaporated, 12 to 15 minutes. Remove from the heat and keep warm.

Fill the tortillas with the jackfruit and top with pico de gallo, vegan crema, avocado (if desired), and cilantro. Serve the tacos with lime wedges for squeezing.

Sweet Potato and Kale Tacos

Sweet potatoes and kale are a super-delicious combo that also happens to be chock-full of vitamins and minerals, and a good amount of protein. So I decided to turn them into a taco filling. Tamari gives a great savory flavor, while the nutritional yeast bumps up the umami factor even more. There's also a smoky kick from chipotle powder.

MAKES 10 TACOS

2 tablespoons avocado oil

1½ pounds sweet potatoes, cut into ½-inch cubes

½ white onion, roughly chopped

4 tablespoons vegetable broth or water, or as needed

2 tablespoons garlic powder

1 tablespoon dried oregano

1 tablespoon ground cumin

1 teaspoon chipotle powder or cayenne pepper

3 tablespoons nutritional yeast (optional)

3 tablespoons tamari

4 cups roughly chopped kale

Fine sea salt

10 corn tortillas (see page 44), warmed

Mango Salsa (page 152) or Salsa al Horno (page 151) for topping

Chopped cilantro leaves and tender stems for topping

Vegan queso fresco (see page 164) for serving (optional)

Lime wedges for squeezing

Set a large saucepan over medium-high heat. Add the avocado oil, sweet potatoes, and onion and cook, stirring, until the sweet potatoes are soft on the outside, about 5 minutes. (If they start sticking to the skillet, stir in a tablespoon or two of the vegetable broth.) Add the garlic powder, oregano, cumin, chipotle powder, nutritional yeast (if using), and 1 to 2 tablespoons of the vegetable broth. Cook, stirring, until the mixture starts to look dry, 3 to 4 minutes. Immediately add the tamari and cook, stirring, until the sweet potatoes are cooked through, about 5 minutes. Stir in another 1 to 2 tablespoons vegetable broth along with the kale.

Remove the skillet from the heat and let the residual heat cook the kale a bit. Add a pinch of salt and stir to combine.

Fill the tortillas with the sweet potato and kale and top with salsa, cilantro, and vegan queso fresco (if desired). Serve the tacos with lime wedges for squeezing.

Taquitos de Camote

Taquitos are like mini chimichangas, and I've never met anyone who didn't like the little fried bundles. They're crispy and usually filled with potatoes and cheese, so I thought sweet potatoes and vegan cream cheese would be great for that sweet-savory component. People go crazy for these taquitos, especially with all the fixin's. You can roll them in advance and fry them later. Serve a few taquitos as an app; or if you're feeling indulgent, serve more for a full meal.

MAKES 16 TAQUITOS

Fine sea salt

4 large sweet potatoes, white or orange, lightly scrubbed and cut into thirds

8 to 10 tablespoons avocado oil

½ yellow onion, roughly chopped

4 garlic cloves, roughly chopped

½ cup vegan cream cheese

2 tablespoons nutritional yeast

1 tablespoon ground cumin

1 tablespoon paprika

16 corn tortillas (see page 44)

Sliced avocado for serving

Shredded green cabbage for serving

Salsa Verde (page 148) for serving

Fermented Vegan Crema (page 163) for serving

Chopped cilantro leaves and tender stems for serving

Cooked beans (see pages 31 to 36) for serving (optional)

Cooked rice (see pages 39 to 43) for serving (optional)

Bring a large pot of water to a boil over high heat and then turn the heat to medium-high. Add a pinch of salt and the sweet potatoes, cover, and cook until a fork easily pierces the potatoes, 25 to 30 minutes. Drain and transfer to a large bowl.

Meanwhile, in a medium skillet over medium heat, warm 1 to 2 tablespoons of the avocado oil. Add the onion and garlic and cook, stirring occasionally, until the onion is translucent, about 6 minutes. Transfer to the large bowl. Add the cream cheese, nutritional yeast, cumin, paprika, and ½ teaspoon salt and mash with a potato masher or fork and mix well. Set this filling aside.

Set a small skillet over medium heat. Add one tortilla at a time and warm, just until you can bend it without breaking, about 15 seconds per side. Add ¼ cup of the filling to each tortilla and roll up like a cigar. (If you have someone helping you, they can warm the tortillas as you roll them.)

In a medium cast-iron skillet over medium heat, warm 1 to 2 tablespoons avocado oil until the oil bubbles around a wooden chopstick when inserted. Add three or four taquitos and cook each side until golden brown and crispy all over, 4 to 6 minutes total. If it seems like the taquitos are browning too quickly, lower the heat. Remove the taquitos and drain on paper towels; keep hot. Continue to cook three or four taquitos at a time, adding more oil for each batch as needed.

Serve the taquitos while still hot with avocado, cabbage, salsa, vegan crema, and cilantro, as well as beans and rice, if desired.

Quesadillas con Plátanos

There was a time when I just couldn't get enough of plantains. I ate them every which way, and one day I got the idea to layer plantains in a quesadilla with spinach. It's a deeply satisfying dish that's super-easy to make. Just be sure your plantains are ripe; otherwise, you'll get a bitter, unpleasant sensation that's worse than eating an unripe banana! For what to look for when choosing ripe plantains, see page 11.

MAKES 4 SERVINGS

3 tablespoons coconut oil

½ white onion, roughly chopped

2 ripe plantains, peeled and halved crosswise

Four 8-inch flour tortillas (see page 47)

1 cup shredded vegan cheese

3 cups baby spinach

Himalayan pink salt

Salsa al Horno (page 151) for serving

Vegan Cilantro Crema (page 159) for serving

Chopped cilantro leaves and tender stems for serving

Warm a medium cast-iron or stainless-steel skillet over medium heat for 5 to 6 minutes. Add 1 tablespoon of the coconut oil and the onion and cook, stirring, until translucent, about 6 minutes. Transfer to a small bowl and set aside.

Turn the heat to medium-low and add the remaining 2 tablespoons coconut oil. Add the plantains and cook each side until caramelized but still firm, about 4 minutes. Don't move them too much or they will get mushy. Transfer to a plate and let cool a bit, then slice into bite-size coins.

While the plantains cool, place one tortilla in the skillet, turn the heat to medium-low, and sprinkle with some of the vegan cheese. Cook until the cheese melts, 4 to 5 minutes. Transfer to a plate. Repeat with the remaining tortillas and cheese.

Remove the skillet from the heat. Add the spinach and about 1 tablespoon water, stir, and let the residual heat cook the spinach.

Fill the tortillas with the plantains, onion, and spinach, then sprinkle each with a pinch of pink salt. Close the quesadillas by folding in half. Serve with salsa, vegan crema, and cilantro to add as desired.

Quesadillas de Brócoli y Tofu

These broccoli and tofu quesadillas take me back to my college days when I practically subsisted on them. They're super-cheap and quick to make. I coat the broccoli and tofu in a tangy tomato-chile sauce. It makes the filling pretty saucy, so, to avoid sogging out the quesadilla, I like to serve it on the side of the cheesy tortilla. When the two mingle, it's magical.

MAKES 2 SERVINGS

2 California chiles

2 guajillo chiles

2 chiles de árbol

2 tablespoons coconut oil

1 pound Roma tomatoes

¼ white onion

1 pound broccoli, cut into bite-size florets

1½ tablespoons white vinegar

3 large garlic cloves

2 teaspoons cane sugar

1 teaspoon fine sea salt

One 14- to 16-ounce package firm tofu, drained and crumbled into large pieces

Four 8-inch flour tortillas (see page 47)

2 to 4 slices vegan cheese

Avocado wedges for serving (optional)

In a small saucepan over high heat, bring 2 cups water to a boil. Add all the chiles, cover, and boil until the chiles become lighter in color and the water is reddish orange, about 8 minutes. Remove from the heat and let the chiles soak, covered, until ready to use, then drain.

Meanwhile, warm a large cast-iron skillet over high heat for 2 to 3 minutes. Add 1 tablespoon of the coconut oil and turn the heat to medium. Add the tomatoes and onion and cook, turning occasionally, until charred all over and squishy to the touch of your tongs, 6 to 8 minutes.

Warm a large stainless-steel skillet over high heat for 2 to 3 minutes. Add the remaining 1 tablespoon coconut oil and turn the heat to medium. Add the broccoli and cook, stirring occasionally, until lightly browned at the edges, 4 to 5 minutes.

By this time, the tomatoes and onion should be done. Transfer them to a high-powered blender; add the vinegar, soaked chiles, garlic, sugar, and salt; and blend until the texture resembles chunky sauce, about 15 seconds. Strain through a medium-mesh sieve into a small saucepan. Turn the heat to high, add the tofu, and bring to a simmer. Turn the heat to medium-low and cook until the sauce thickens, 8 to 10 minutes. Pour the sauce over the broccoli and stir well to combine.

Set the same cast-iron skillet over high heat until hot, about 3 minutes. Turn the heat to medium-low, add two tortillas, and cook on one side until warm, 3 to 4 minutes. Flip and top one of the tortillas with a slice or two of cheese. Top with the second tortilla, cooked-side down, and cook until the cheese is melted, flipping halfway through. Repeat with the remaining tortillas and cheese.

You can either open the quesadilla and fill with the broccoli and sauce mixture or serve them side by side, with avocado wedges, if desired.

Quesadillas de Fajitas

This dish is exactly what it sounds like: sautéed onions and peppers inside quesadillas. My mom first made these when I came to visit from college. She had prepared another dish for me but it had chicken broth, which she didn't realize I couldn't eat, so she cobbled together these quesadillas as a last-minute fix. Luckily, she had vegan cheese that I'd left in the fridge from my previous visit. Once again, my mom came to the rescue with her resourcefulness.

MAKES 4 SERVINGS

2 tablespoons avocado oil, plus more for drizzling

4 garlic cloves, minced

1 jalapeño chile, minced

1 white onion, halved and sliced ½ inch thick

2 poblano chiles, seeded and sliced ½ inch thick

1 bell pepper, any color, seeded and sliced ½ inch thick

¼ teaspoon ground turmeric

½ teaspoon fine sea salt

½ teaspoon freshly ground black pepper

8 flour tortillas (see page 47)

8 slices vegan cheese

Avocado Salsa (page 155) or any salsa of your choice for topping

Fermented Vegan Crema (page 163) for topping

Chopped cilantro leaves and tender stems for topping

Warm a large stainless-steel skillet over low heat for 2 to 3 minutes. Add the 2 tablespoons avocado oil, garlic, and jalapeño and cook, stirring, until fragrant, 2 to 3 minutes. Add the onion, poblanos, bell pepper, turmeric, salt, and black pepper; turn the heat to medium-low; and cook, tossing or stirring frequently to prevent burning, until the onion is slightly golden, 6 to 8 minutes. Remove from the heat and set these fajitas aside.

Set another skillet over medium heat and drizzle in some avocado oil. Add one tortilla, top with two slices of the cheese, and then stack another tortilla on top. Cook, checking on the tortilla to make sure it's not burning, until a bit brown and crisp, 3 to 4 minutes. Flip and cook the other side until a bit brown and crisp, 2 to 3 minutes more. Repeat with the remaining tortillas and cheese to finish the quesadillas.

Serve the quesadillas with the fajitas tucked inside, or on the side, and top with salsa, vegan crema, and cilantro, if desired.

Papas Chorreadas

People often associate potatoes with Ireland, but don't sleep on Colombia! That country grows lots of potatoes, and the people sure know how to cook them up. This dish, for instance, is a must at any Colombian party. The potatoes are boiled and then smothered with a sweet and tangy sauce that spreads like . . . well, something you don't want to think about while eating. So let me just say, ask a Spanish-speaking friend what "chorreadas" means. But be prepared for some serious side-eye.

MAKES 6 SERVINGS

12 medium Yukon gold potatoes, scrubbed

6 Roma tomatoes

3 tablespoons avocado oil

1 white onion, finely chopped

4 large garlic cloves, minced

1 tablespoon white vinegar

1 tablespoon grated panela (unrefined Mexican brown sugar, also known as piloncillo) or packed dark brown sugar (optional)

1 teaspoon fine sea salt

Freshly ground black pepper

Sliced green onions for serving (optional)

Bring a large pot of water to a boil over high heat. Add the potatoes (make sure there's enough water to cover them by 2 inches) and boil until tender and fully cooked, 15 to 20 minutes. Drain and keep warm.

Meanwhile, bring a medium saucepan of water to a boil. Using a paring knife, score a shallow X on the bottom of each tomato. Fill a large bowl with ice cubes and water; set aside.

Working with one tomato at a time, place each in the boiling water until the skin at the X starts to peel, about 30 seconds. Using a spider or slotted spoon, transfer the tomato to the prepared ice bath. When cool enough to handle, peel the tomatoes and finely chop. Discard the peels.

Set a medium stainless-steel skillet over medium heat. Add the avocado oil, white onion, garlic, and tomatoes; bring to a simmer; and cook, stirring, until the tomato pieces start to break down and are incorporated with the other ingredients, about 15 minutes. Add the vinegar; if your tomatoes aren't ripe and sweet, add the sugar. Cook, stirring, until saucy, about 5 minutes. Remove from the heat and stir in the salt.

Spoon the sauce over the boiled potatoes, sprinkle with pepper and green onions (if desired), and serve.

Chiles Rellenos

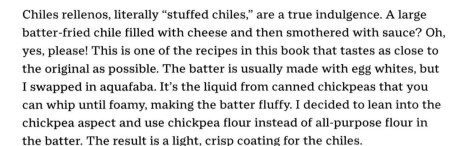

Chiles rellenos, literally "stuffed chiles," are a true indulgence. A large batter-fried chile filled with cheese and then smothered with sauce? Oh, yes, please! This is one of the recipes in this book that tastes as close to the original as possible. The batter is usually made with egg whites, but I swapped in aquafaba. It's the liquid from canned chickpeas that you can whip until foamy, making the batter fluffy. I decided to lean into the chickpea aspect and use chickpea flour instead of all-purpose flour in the batter. The result is a light, crisp coating for the chiles.

MAKES 6 TO 8 SERVINGS

CREAMY TOMATO SAUCE

3 large Roma tomatoes, cored

2 serrano chiles, stemmed and seeded (use gloves!)

¼ white onion, quartered

3 large garlic cloves, quartered

½ cup raw cashew pieces, soaked in water to cover for 24 hours (or boiled for 15 minutes) and then drained

1½ cups low-sodium vegetable broth

½ teaspoon fine sea salt

CHICKPEA BATTER

1½ cups packed chickpea flour

1 tablespoon granulated garlic (see Note, page 60)

½ teaspoon ground turmeric

½ teaspoon fine sea salt

½ teaspoon freshly ground black pepper

¾ cup plus 1 tablespoon aquafaba (liquid from a 15.5-ounce can chickpeas)

6 to 8 poblano chiles, charred, peeled, and cooled (see page 178)

Avocado oil for frying

One 12-ounce block vegan cheddar or mozzarella, cut crosswise into ⅓-inch-thick slices

Frijoles Fritos (page 103) for serving

Cilantro Rice (page 40) for serving

Vegan queso fresco (see page 164) for serving

To make the sauce: In a high-powered blender, combine the tomatoes, serranos, onion, garlic, cashews, vegetable broth, and salt and blend on high speed until creamy, about 2 minutes. Transfer to a large pot over medium-low heat and simmer for 10 minutes. Keep warm.

To make the batter: In a medium bowl, whisk together the chickpea flour, granulated garlic, turmeric, salt, and black pepper. Transfer 1 cup (gently packed) of the mixture to a large plate and spread out well.

In a large bowl, beat the aquafaba with a handheld mixer or electric whisk on medium speed until completely frothy, 4 to 5 minutes. Add ¼ cup of the remaining chickpea flour mixture and mix on high speed until completely incorporated into the aquafaba. Repeat with the remaining chickpea flour mixture.

CONTINUED

Using a paring knife, cut a slit in one side of each poblano and remove the seeds.

Warm a nonstick skillet over medium-high heat for 3 to 4 minutes, then add 2 tablespoons avocado oil. Tuck three slices of cheese inside each poblano and dredge in the chickpea flour mixture on the plate, covering the whole chile. Now dip the poblano in the batter and place in the hot skillet. Immediately spoon in ample batter to spread over the poblano. Cover, turn the heat to medium-low, and cook until golden brown and crisp on the bottom, 3 to 4 minutes. Flip the poblano, cover, and fry for 1 minute more. Transfer the poblano to a plate. Repeat with the remaining poblanos, frying them one at a time and adding 1 tablespoon avocado oil as needed.

Top the fried chiles with the creamy tomato sauce. Serve immediately with beans, rice, and vegan queso fresco.

Hongos a la Diabla

◇

This dish is based on camarones a la diabla, "deviled shrimp." The sour-savory chile flavor of the sauce complements lion's mane mushrooms. If you can't find lion's mane, substitute oyster mushrooms. As the name suggests, this one will make you sweat and cry—but in a good way! If you really have to, cut back to just two chiles. Don't omit them, though. The dish just won't taste the same.

MAKES 4 TO 6 SERVINGS

8 guajillo chiles

2 to 4 chiles de árbol (depending on heat preference)

2 tablespoons avocado oil, plus more for drizzling

3 large vine-ripened tomatoes (preferably Tasti-Lee), roughly chopped

3 garlic cloves, or 2 teaspoons granulated garlic (see Note, page 60)

⅓ cup fresh orange juice

2 tablespoons white vinegar

1 teaspoon fine sea salt

2¼ pounds lion's mane mushrooms

½ white or yellow onion, sliced

Frijoles Colombianos (page 36) for serving

Cooked rice (see pages 39 to 43) for serving

Ensalada de Nopales (page 177) for serving

Corn tortillas (see page 44) for serving

Finely chopped cilantro leaves and tender stems for garnish

Vegan queso fresco (see page 164) for garnish

Pop the stems off the guajillos and chiles de árbol and rip the chiles open a bit until you can shake out and discard the seeds.

Warm a small saucepan over medium-low heat for 2 to 3 minutes, then turn the heat to low. Add the 2 tablespoons avocado oil and the chiles and cook, stirring gently, until they puff up and take on a golden red color, 5 to 6 minutes. If the chiles start to brown, immediately remove the pan from the heat and try again at a lower temperature. It's important not to brown the chiles because they get bitter. Remove the pan from the heat and transfer the chiles to a plate, shaking any excess oil back into the pan.

Add the tomatoes to the same saucepan, turn the heat to medium-low, and cook until slightly saucy, 3 to 4 minutes. Remove from the heat and transfer to a high-powered blender. Add the garlic, orange juice, vinegar, salt, and cooled chiles. Blend until smooth and completely emulsified, 30 to 45 seconds, and set this sauce aside.

Warm a large cast-iron skillet over medium heat for 2 to 3 minutes. Drizzle in about 2 teaspoons avocado oil, then add some of each of the mushrooms and onion, making sure you don't overcrowd the skillet. Cook until the mushrooms are crispy and golden, flipping gently once, 3 to 4 minutes per side. (At first, the mushrooms should be plump, then at around 2 minutes, they should release their liquid. At around 6 minutes, the liquid should have cooked off.) If the mushrooms are browning too quickly, lower the heat and flip immediately. Remove to a plate and repeat with additional avocado oil and the remaining mushrooms and onion.

Return all the mushrooms and onion to the skillet. Strain the sauce through a fine-mesh sieve over the skillet; discard the solids. Simmer over medium heat, stirring occasionally to prevent sticking, until thickened, about 6 minutes.

Serve the mushrooms with the beans, rice, salad, and tortillas on the side, and garnish with cilantro and vegan queso fresco.

Elote Asado

—⬦—

Just as you may see elote offered at street fairs in the United States, it's also a popular street-vendor food in Mexico. Who can resist grilled corn slathered with crema and sprinkled with bold spices? Some vendors add novel toppings, such as crushed potato chips. But the classic way is with chili powder, lime, and a spicy dried-chile salsa. I make a vegan Cotija cheese for the elote that's just killer. You don't have to wait for the street fair anymore to have Mexican street corn!

MAKES 8 SERVINGS

8 ears corn, shucked

1 cup vegan mayonnaise

¾ cup Vegan Cotija Cheese (page 92), crumbled

1 cup finely chopped cilantro leaves and tender stems

Lime wedges for squeezing

Cooked beans (see pages 31 to 36) for serving (optional)

Cooked rice (see pages 39 to 43) for serving (optional)

Bring a large pot of water to a boil. Add the corn, boil for 5 minutes, and then drain.

Meanwhile, prepare a charcoal grill for high-heat cooking and add some hickory wood chunks to get their smoky flavor, then wait 15 to 20 minutes to achieve a medium-low heat. Place the boiled corn on the grates and grill, turning occasionally, until you see some charred marks, 5 to 7 minutes.

Remove the corn from the heat, slather with the mayonnaise, and then sprinkle with the Cotija and cilantro before squeezing lime juice over all. Serve with beans and rice, if desired.

VARIATION

If you like, you can skip firing up the grill and simply steam the corn until tender, 7 to 10 minutes, then top as directed. Or for a smokier flavor, steam the corn for 5 minutes, then grill in a preheated grill pan over medium heat, turning occasionally, until you see some charred marks. (Or char the corn nicely in some areas with a culinary torch.)

Vegan Cotija Cheese

Traditional dairy Cotija cheese is dry and crumbly, similar in texture to some kinds of feta. It's salty and actually pretty pungent. In fact, we call Cotija "foot or paw cheese." I make a vegan version that's a bit milder, with unsoaked macadamia nuts to keep the cheese firm and fluffy. So when you sprinkle this Cotija on Mexican street corn, it will stay on the cobs.

MAKES ABOUT 8 OUNCES

1½ cups blanched (no skin) macadamia nuts or almonds

¼ cup pickle juice or white vinegar

2 tablespoons fresh lemon juice

1 tablespoon granulated garlic (see Note, page 60)

1 tablespoon nutritional yeast

½ teaspoon fine sea salt

Preheat the oven to 350°F with a rack in the center position.

In a high-powered blender, pulse the nuts until crumbly and the texture resembles coarse sea salt. Transfer to a large rimmed baking sheet; sprinkle with the pickle juice, lemon juice, garlic, nutritional yeast, and salt; and mix well with your hands. Spread evenly in a single layer and bake for 17 minutes. Remove from the oven and use a spatula to mix the nuts, then spread evenly once again and bake until browned and dry, about 17 minutes more.

Remove the Cojita from the oven and let cool and dry completely, about 30 minutes. Store in a glass jar in the refrigerator for up to 3 weeks.

Coliflor Asada

A whole head of roasted cauliflower on the table is as impressive as any meat roast. My mom and I actually made this dish together for vegan Thanksgiving. People who claim not to like cauliflower often change their tune when it's roasted. It becomes sweeter and pretty irresistible, especially when combined with the spiced almond butter sauce. This easy-to-prepare dish is great on its own and also plays nicely with other dishes on the table, like Ensalada de Nopales (page 177), Frijoles Colombianos (page 36), Arroz con Coco (page 104), and Avocado Salsa (page 155).

MAKES 6 SERVINGS

1 head cauliflower, leaves removed

⅓ cup almond butter

2 tablespoons avocado oil

2 tablespoons yellow or Dijon mustard

Juice of 1 lime, plus lime wedges for squeezing

1 tablespoon ground cumin

1 tablespoon smoked paprika

1 tablespoon granulated garlic (see Note, page 60)

Fine sea salt

⅓ cup chopped cilantro leaves and tender stems

Freshly ground black pepper

Vegan Cilantro Crema (page 159) for serving

Preheat the oven to 350°F. Line a 9 by 13-inch baking pan with parchment paper.

Bring a large pot of water to a boil. Add the cauliflower and boil until semi-tender but not super-soft, 5 to 7 minutes. Drain the cauliflower and rinse with cold water; drain again and set aside.

In a medium bowl, combine the almond butter, avocado oil, mustard, lime juice, cumin, paprika, granulated garlic, and ½ teaspoon salt; whisk with a fork until well combined. Taste and season with additional salt, if necessary.

Place the cauliflower in the prepared baking pan and top with the almond butter sauce, brushing it all over with a silicone brush or spatula.

Bake the cauliflower until tender and charred in spots, about 20 minutes.

Sprinkle the cauliflower with the cilantro and black pepper, squeeze lime wedges over the top, and serve with cilantro crema.

Guisado de Papa y Nopales

When I turned vegetarian as a teenager, my mom cooked this potato and cactus guisado for me all the time. It's a hearty stew that's traditionally made with beef, but she added more potatoes instead. The nopales, otherwise known as prickly pear cactus pads, aren't traditional at all, but they add such great texture and flavor.

When I would take guisado to school, everyone would get envious of my lunch. So I started taking it in a bigger container to share—and ended up with not much for myself! I didn't mind, though. I enjoyed sharing food with my friends, and it made me pretty popular!

MAKES 6 TO 8 SERVINGS

About 1 pound nopales (see Note)

¼ white onion, plus ½ onion chopped

4 garlic cloves; 3 minced

½ teaspoon fine sea salt

2 tablespoons avocado oil

3 Yukon gold potatoes, cut into ½-inch cubes

4 Roma tomatoes, roughly chopped

2 teaspoons ground cumin

⅛ teaspoon ground turmeric

1½ teaspoons Himalayan pink salt

Freshly ground black pepper

Arroz con Coco (page 104) for serving

Frijoles Fritos (page 103) for serving

Maduros (page 136) for serving (optional)

Vegan Cojita cheese (see page 92) for sprinkling (optional)

Bring a medium pot of water to a boil; there should be enough water to cover the nopales.

Meanwhile, trim off the sides and thorns from the nopales, if necessary, running a sharp knife back and forth over the surface until completely clean. Cut the nopales lengthwise into strips, then cut crosswise into bite-size pieces. Transfer to the boiling water. Add the ¼ onion, whole garlic clove, and sea salt and boil until the nopales are tender, watching closely, about 10 minutes. (The nopales will exude a sticky fluid, similar to okra, and may foam up. If this happens, lower the heat and add a little avocado oil to prevent the pot from overflowing.) Drain in a fine-mesh sieve and rinse with cold water; discard the onion and garlic. Set aside in the sieve to continue to drain.

Warm a large stainless-steel skillet over medium heat for 2 to 3 minutes. Add the avocado oil and chopped onion and cook, stirring often, until the onion is translucent and slightly browned, 3 to 4 minutes. Add the potatoes and minced garlic and cook, stirring constantly to prevent sticking, until the garlic is fragrant and the potatoes start to change color, 4 to 5 minutes. Add the tomatoes, nopales, cumin, turmeric, pink salt, and a pinch of pepper and cook, stirring constantly, until the potatoes are tender, about 10 minutes more.

Serve the guisado with rice, beans, and maduros (if desired) on the side, and sprinkle with vegan Cojita (if desired).

NOTE You may be able to find the nopales at a Latin market already dethorned, sliced, and cooked. Cut them into bite-size pieces, if necessary, for this recipe. You'll need 3½ cups. Proceed with cooking in the skillet as directed.

Guisado de Garbanzos

———◇———

Inspired by Colombian guisado, these stewy chickpeas in a tangy tomato broth are great with Colombian beans and rice. I simmer the chickpeas with a charred nectarine, which is pretty unconventional. You can't taste the fruit in the final dish, but it amplifies the flavors of the jalapeño and tomatoes. Reserve the chickpea liquid, aka aquafaba, for another use, such as Chiles Rellenos, page 85.

MAKES 4 SERVINGS

2 large vine-ripened tomatoes (preferably Tasti-Lee)

2 tomatillos, husked

1 large jalapeño chile

1 nectarine, halved and pitted

2 garlic cloves

1 tablespoon paprika

2 teaspoons ground cumin

1 teaspoon fine sea salt

3 tablespoons avocado oil

¼ white onion, thinly sliced

Two 15.5-ounce cans chickpeas, drained

Cilantro Rice (page 40) for serving

Frijoles Colombianos (page 36) for serving

Bring a medium saucepan of water to a boil. Meanwhile, using a paring knife, score a shallow X on the bottom of each tomato and tomatillo. Fill a large bowl with ice and water; set aside.

Working with one tomato or tomatillo at a time, place in the boiling water until the skin at the X starts to peel, about 30 seconds. Using a spider or slotted spoon, transfer to the prepared ice bath and let cool. Peel and finely chop the flesh and transfer to a high-powered blender. Discard the peels.

Set a medium cast-iron or stainless-steel skillet over medium heat. Add the jalapeño and nectarine and cook, flipping occasionally, until charred all over, 6 to 8 minutes. Transfer to a plate and let cool completely, then stem the jalapeño. Transfer to the blender; add the garlic, paprika, cumin, and salt; and blend until smooth, about 1 minute. Set this salsa aside.

In a large nonstick skillet over medium heat, warm the avocado oil. Add the onion and cook, stirring occasionally, until translucent, about 4 minutes. Add the chickpeas and cook for 5 minutes more. Add the salsa, cover, turn the heat to medium-low, and simmer until the broth is thickened and stewy, about 15 minutes. Remove from the heat and let sit, covered, for 5 minutes.

Serve the guisado with rice and beans on the side.

Jackfruit Tinga Tostadas

—◇—

Tinga is both fun to say and easy to make! It's a tomato-based dish, popular in Central Mexico, that involves a variety of spices, onions, and chipotle chiles in adobo sauce. It's usually made with shredded chicken, but I use young (green) jackfruit, which mimics the texture of chicken when shredded. Also, remember not to add too many chipotle chiles (my past experience of adding an entire can was regretful). A little goes a long way, even for my spice-forward family.

MAKES 8 TO 10 TOSTADAS

2 tablespoons avocado oil

1 large yellow onion, diced

Two 14-ounce cans young (green) jackfruit in water, rinsed and drained

4 large tomatoes, cored and roughly chopped

6 garlic cloves

¼ cup vegetable broth

2 chipotle chiles in adobo sauce, plus 2 tablespoons sauce from the can, or 4 dried chipotle chiles soaked overnight in ⅓ cup water and stemmed, plus the soaking liquid

1 tablespoon coconut sugar

1 tablespoon apple cider vinegar

2 teaspoons ground cumin

2 teaspoons fine sea salt

1 teaspoon freshly ground black pepper

8 to 10 tostadas

Chopped cilantro leaves and tender stems for topping

Shredded green cabbage for topping

Vegan crema (see pages 159 to 163) for topping

In a medium nonstick pot over medium heat, warm the avocado oil. Add the onion and cook, stirring occasionally, until transparent, about 7 minutes. Meanwhile, shred the jackfruit, leaving some bigger pieces. Add it to the pot, turn the heat to medium-high, and cook, stirring frequently, for about 10 minutes. If the jackfruit starts to stick to the pot, stir in 1 to 2 tablespoons water. Remove from the heat.

In a high-powered blender, combine the tomatoes, garlic, vegetable broth, and chipotle chiles with sauce or soaking liquid and blend to a slightly chunky consistency.

Add the chipotle-tomato sauce to the jackfruit, set over medium heat, and bring to a simmer. Add the coconut sugar, vinegar, cumin, salt, and pepper; stir well; turn the heat to low; and simmer until most of the liquid has evaporated and the tinga has the consistency of a salsa, about 25 minutes.

Spoon the jackfruit tinga on the tostadas and top with cilantro, cabbage, and vegan crema before serving.

Frijoles Fritos

I hope this isn't news to you, but refried beans are traditionally made with lard. I give them a vegan makeover with coconut manna. Manna is similar to a coconut butter and has that *creeeeaminess* that lard would bring. It really changes the flavor of the beans. Manna is heat sensitive and must be cooked on low to preserve the flavor. You could serve these beans with virtually any dish, but I particularly like them with Chiles Rellenos (page 85), Hongos a la Diabla (page 88), quesadillas (see pages 75 to 81), and chilaquiles (see pages 125 and 126).

MAKES 8 SERVINGS

3 tablespoons coconut manna (see Note) or coconut oil

4 to 6 chiles de árbol or dried Japanese chiles (depending on heat preference)

1 large garlic clove

4 cups cooked pinto beans in cooking liquid (see page 31), or three 15.5-ounce cans pinto beans; one can rinsed and drained

1 teaspoon fine sea salt

Warm a large skillet over medium heat for 3 to 4 minutes. Add the coconut manna, dried chiles, and garlic; turn the heat to low; and cook, stirring, until the chiles and garlic are dark brown, about 5 minutes. Lower the heat if it starts to burn (you'll see steam). Using a slotted spoon, remove and discard the chiles and garlic, leaving the oil in the skillet.

Add the beans and liquid to the skillet and mash with a potato masher, leaving half the beans whole, then bring to a boil and cook for 6 to 8 minutes. Season with salt before serving.

NOTE Coconut manna, also known as coconut butter, is creamier and richer than coconut oil. The manna is made from processing coconut flesh (not just extracting the oil from the flesh).

Arroz con Coco

This rice with coconut flakes was inspired by a dish that I had in Cartegena, Columbia. It's a great side for any entrée, especially spicy ones with some sauce, like my Hongos a la Diabla (page 88) and Pipian (page 23). This recipe is super-simple, yet so delicious. The sweet-savory combo is extremely satisfying; I can practically eat this rice all on its own.

The rice can be prepared up to 5 days in advance and stored in an airtight container in the refrigerator. When ready to serve, put it in a small saucepan over medium-low heat with about ¼ cup water. Cover and cook until the rice is warm and has absorbed all the liquid.

MAKES 8 TO 10 SERVINGS

2 cups long-grain jasmine rice

3 tablespoons coconut oil

½ medium white onion, finely chopped

3 large garlic cloves, minced

½ cup unsweetened coconut flakes

2½ cups water

2 cups vegetable broth

1 teaspoon fine sea salt

Thoroughly rinse the rice in a fine-mesh sieve under running water until the water is clear. Drain in the sieve for 10 minutes.

In a large pot with a tight-fitting lid over high heat, warm the coconut oil. Turn the heat to medium; add the onion, garlic, and coconut flakes; and cook, stirring, until the onion is semi-translucent and the coconut is toasted brown, about 5 minutes. Add the rice and cook, stirring well, until the rice is toasted brown but not burnt, 6 to 8 minutes. Add the 2½ cups water, vegetable broth, and salt and stir well. Bring to a boil, then cover and turn the heat to medium-low. Cook until the rice is tender and the liquid is absorbed, about 15 minutes. Serve warm.

Arepas de Maiz con Aguacate

These Colombian-style arepas are made with kernels of sweet corn in the dough. Also called arepas de chocolo, they're softer and fluffier (like small pancakes) than their sturdier Venezuelan counterparts. I started making these sweet corn cakes at home because I was craving them but no place nearby sold them. I consulted with my partner's Colombian mom for the recipe, so they're legit. I load up the arepas with my favorite toppings. It's like a fancy avocado toast, but on gluten-free arepa instead of bread.

MAKES 8 SERVINGS

AVOCADO SPREAD
2 ripe avocados, pitted and peeled

2 tablespoons fresh lime juice

1 teaspoon garlic powder

1 pinch fine sea salt

1 pinch freshly ground black pepper

AREPAS
1½ cups instant corn masa flour (such as Maseca)

3 tablespoons nutritional yeast

½ teaspoon Himalayan pink salt

Two 15-ounce cans sweet corn, rinsed and drained

Avocado oil for frying

½ cup cilantro leaves

Maple syrup for topping

Frijoles Fritos (page 103) for topping (optional)

Hongos a la Diabla (page 88) for topping (optional)

Vegan queso fresco (see page 164) for topping (optional)

1 red bell pepper, finely diced (optional)

Diced white onion for topping (optional)

To make the spread: In a high-powered blender or food processor, combine the avocados, lime juice, garlic powder, sea salt, and black pepper and blend on high speed until fluffy and smooth, about 45 seconds. (Alternatively, combine the ingredients in a bowl and mash with a fork until smooth.) Transfer to a bowl and set aside.

To make the arepas: In a small bowl, whisk together the masa, nutritional yeast, and pink salt. Set aside.

In the blender, blend the corn on high speed until mostly smooth with some small chunks, about 30 seconds. Transfer to a medium bowl, add the masa mixture, ½ cup at a time, and combine with your hands until a moist dough, the consistency of soft Play-Doh, forms. Set aside.

Set a large nonstick skillet over medium-low heat and drizzle with a little avocado oil. Using your hands, form the arepa dough into thick disks—you can use a ⅓-cup measure if you want the arepas to be a uniform size. Working in batches, add the arepas to the skillet and cook until firm to the touch and brown spots appear, 5 to 6 minutes on each side. Lower the heat if they brown too quickly.

Once you cook all of the arepas, you can start serving. Using a silicone spatula or offset spatula, smear some of the avocado spread on top of each arepa, then top with the cilantro and maple syrup and beans, mushrooms, vegan queso fresco, bell pepper, and onion, as desired. Enjoy.

Vegan Queso Fundido

This is my vegan take on queso fundido, a skillet of gooey molten cheese that's always a crowd fave. Here, the pre-pressed tofu gets really crumbly when you fry and press on it. Then as the tofu simmers in the tomato sauce, it softens up. The sauce is garnished with a handful of fresh basil—that combo may seem more Italian than Mexican but this is how my mom makes her queso, and I've always loved the flavors.

MAKES 4 TO 5 APPETIZER SERVINGS

One 16-ounce package extra-firm pre-pressed tofu

1 tablespoon avocado oil

1 pound Roma tomatoes

4 large garlic cloves

1 tablespoon white wine vinegar

1 teaspoon Himalayan pink salt

1 pinch freshly ground black pepper

1 handful basil leaves

Cilantro Rice (page 40) for serving

Frijoles Fritos (page 103) for serving

On a cutting board, stand the tofu on one of its long sides. Slice in thirds straight down from the top to create three slabs, each about 1 inch thick. Lay these slabs flat and slice each in thirds from the top. You should have nine pieces of tofu, each measuring about 1 by 1½ by 3 inches.

Warm a large cast-iron skillet over high heat for 3 to 4 minutes, then turn the heat to medium. After 1 minute, add the avocado oil and let warm. Add the tofu, spacing the slices apart, and fry, pressing on them, until golden brown, about 5 minutes per side. Transfer to a plate and set aside.

Meanwhile, bring a medium saucepan of water to a boil. Using a paring knife, score a shallow X on the bottom of each tomato. Fill a large bowl with ice and water; set aside.

Working with one tomato at a time, place each in the boiling water until the skin at the X starts to peel, about 30 seconds. Using a spider or slotted spoon, transfer the tomato to the prepared ice bath and let cool. Peel the tomatoes and halve. Discard the peels.

In a high-powered blender, combine the tomatoes, garlic, vinegar, pink salt, and pepper and roughly blend on medium-low speed until smooth, 15 to 20 seconds. Do not overblend, or it will change the flavor.

In a large stainless-steel skillet over medium heat, combine the sauce and tofu and bring to a simmer. Simmer until the sauce thickens and the tofu becomes reddish orange, 15 to 20 minutes.

Serve the tofu garnished with the basil, with a side of rice and beans.

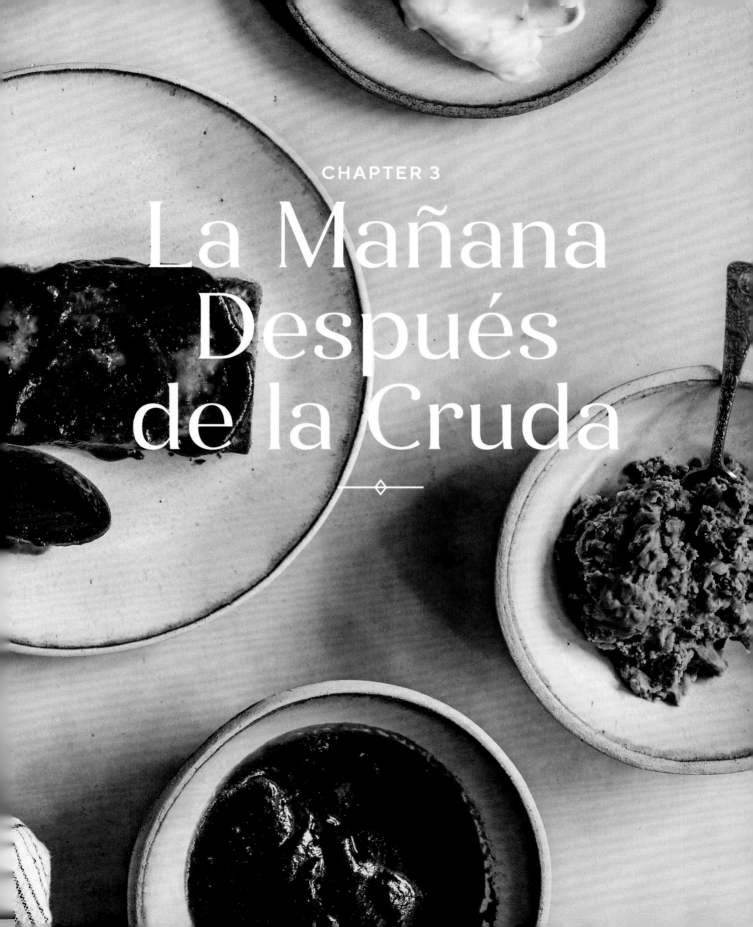

CHAPTER 3

La Mañana Después de la Cruda

The mornings after a fiesta or holiday during my childhood, I remember opening my eyes as the aroma of hot chocolate and the sound of tortillas being made woke me from my sleep. As I went into the kitchen, the table would already be filled with leftovers from dinner the night before and whatever else my abuelita cooked up while we were all asleep—usually fresh salsas, chilaquiles, and arepas.

In my family, a delicious "morning after" follows every celebration. This tradition is both indulgent and practical. My grandmother loves spoiling us with a big breakfast the morning after a holiday, and a morning-after party also ensures that not a single leftover goes to waste.

In a Mexican kitchen, there are always leftover beans, rice, and tortillas that can be turned into breakfast. There are always fresh tomatoes and onions that can be chopped up for salsa. There might also be dishes that were cooked and set aside because they taste better the next day, like menudo. Mexican breakfasts usually include something sweet too—maybe a stack of cinnamon pancakes or gorditas with salsa, and always a mug of hot chocolate.

During the week, breakfast wasn't quite as elaborate but it was just as delicious. When I was a kid, my alarm clock was often the distinctive smell of breakfast burritos cooking in a skillet. My mom and aunts would send me off to school holding several tortillas stuffed with scrambled eggs, beans, salsa, and cilantro.

La Mañana Después de la Cruda is about the anticipation of something good happening, even after the party is over. It's about expressing gratitude for the little things that bring comfort to our lives and the happiness we feel when we're taking care of others.

Burritos de Desayuno

My favorite breakfast as a child was breakfast burritos. Sometimes, I took as many as four mini burritos to school. My mom and aunts had an assembly line—one cooking, one wrapping, and one cleaning.

Those breakfast burritos were filled with pinto beans, scrambled eggs, pico de gallo, avocado, cheese, and loads of ketchup. But now my favorite filling is chickpea and turmeric "eggs." The eggs are flavored with kala namak salt, a Himalayan black salt that imparts a savory flavor similar to hard-boiled egg yolks. You can find it at specialty shops and online.

MAKES 6 BURRITOS

CHICKPEA-TURMERIC SCRAMBLE

½ cup chickpea flour

1 tablespoon garlic powder

1 teaspoon onion powder

½ teaspoon ground turmeric

¼ teaspoon Himalayan pink salt or fine sea salt

Kala namak salt (Himalayan black salt)

1 pinch freshly ground black pepper

½ cup unsweetened almond milk

2 tablespoons avocado oil

2 tablespoons water

Avocado oil for drizzling

Six 6- to 8-inch flour tortillas (see page 47)

1 cup shredded vegan cheese

1 cup Frijoles de la Olla (page 31)

Pico de Gallo (page 147) for serving

1 or 2 avocados, pitted, peeled, and thinly sliced

6 lettuce leaves (optional)

Ketchup for serving

To make the scramble: In a medium bowl, whisk together the chickpea flour, garlic powder, onion powder, turmeric, pink salt, ¼ teaspoon kala namak salt, and black pepper. In another medium bowl, whisk together the almond milk, 1 tablespoon of the avocado oil, and water. Slowly add the dry ingredients to the wet and whisk together. The mixture should have a smooth, runny texture that pours like pancake batter. Set the mixture aside.

In a medium nonstick skillet over medium heat, warm the remaining 1 tablespoon avocado oil. Pour in the mixture and cook, stirring constantly and pressing down with a silicone spatula to flatten, until the mixture resembles scrambled eggs and is a bit crispy, about 10 minutes.

Sprinkle additional kala namak salt on top of the mixture, if desired, and stir once more to incorporate. Remove from the heat and cover.

In another nonstick skillet over medium heat, warm a drizzle of avocado oil. Add a tortilla and cook until golden, about 30 seconds per side. Sprinkle with some of the vegan cheese and cook until the cheese melts. Transfer the tortilla to a plate and add a spoonful each of the scramble, beans, pico de gallo; some of the avocado and a lettuce leaf (if desired); and a little ketchup. Fold the right and left sides of the tortilla toward the middle. Fold the edge closest to you snugly over the filling and continue to roll up the burrito. Repeat with the remaining tortillas and fillings and then serve.

"Huevos" Rancheros

———◇———

I see a lot of variations of huevos rancheros, or ranch-style eggs, but the absolute musts for me are eggs with tomatoes, tortillas, and avocado—the usual suspects in a lot of Mexican recipes. That's what's brilliant about Mexican cooking: We can take the same ingredients and spin them into different dishes that taste distinct. When I was growing up, we ate huevos rancheros a lot because it was easy to make in the morning since we already had the beans prepared. Instead of fried eggs, I add the Chickpea-Turmeric Scramble from my breakfast burritos.

MAKES 3 SERVINGS

1 tablespoon avocado oil

3 corn tortillas (see page 44) or flour tortillas (see page 47)

1 recipe Chickpea-Turmeric Scramble (see page 115)

1 large tomato, diced

¼ white onion, minced

1 avocado, pitted and sliced

Black Beans (see page 135) for serving

Salsa (see pages 147 to 156) for serving

Warm a large cast-iron skillet over high heat for 2 to 3 minutes. Turn the heat to medium and add the avocado oil and tortillas and fry gently on both sides until lightly browned.

Place one tortilla on each plate and top with some of the scramble. Garnish with a generous helping of tomato, onion, and avocado. Finish with a spoonful each of beans and salsa before serving.

Papas con Chorizo Vegano

I *had* to include this recipe in this book because the original was the dish that helped me survive high school. I never liked the school lunches, so my mom made papas con chorizo in bulk and I'd take it to school to share. It actually helped me make friends. It also fueled my passion for sharing food with people.

Back then, my mom would add chorizo made by a local butcher. The flavor memory of that sausage inspired this vegan take with tofu. The sausage is loose, so you don't need to worry about the casings.

MAKES 4 TO 6 SERVINGS

1 pound Yukon gold potatoes, scrubbed and quartered

1 tablespoon white wine vinegar

2 teaspoons fine sea salt

VEGAN CHORIZO

24 ounces firm pre-pressed tofu (see Notes, pages 20 and 120), crumbled

1 tablespoon tomato paste

1 tablespoon white wine vinegar

1 teaspoon paprika

1 teaspoon salt-free all-purpose seasoning

1 teaspoon fine sea salt

1 teaspoon ground cumin

¼ teaspoon dried oregano

⅛ teaspoon cayenne pepper

1 pinch freshly ground black pepper

1 teeny-tiny pinch ground cinnamon

1 Roma tomato, roughly chopped

4 to 5 tablespoons vegetable broth or water

2 tablespoons avocado oil

½ white onion, finely chopped

2 garlic cloves, minced or pressed in a garlic press

Cooked rice (see pages 39 to 43) for serving

Cooked vegan egg substitute for serving

Salsa (see pages 147 to 156) for serving

Vegan crema (see pages 156 to 163) for serving

Avocado wedges for serving (optional)

Chopped cilantro leaves and tender stems for serving (optional)

In a medium saucepan, combine the potatoes, vinegar, and salt and add just enough water to cover. Set over high heat and boil until the potatoes can be pierced with a fork but are still quite firm, about 15 minutes, then drain and cut into bite-size pieces. Set aside.

To make the vegan chorizo: Meanwhile, in a medium bowl, combine the tofu, tomato paste, vinegar, paprika, all-purpose seasoning, salt, cumin, oregano, cayenne, black pepper, and cinnamon. With clean hands, massage and mix all the seasonings into the tofu until evenly combined; the tofu should look like small crumbles that are an even, light orangey brown color. Transfer to a small saucepan.

CONTINUED

Place the chopped tomato in a high-powered blender and blend until smooth, then pour into the saucepan. Set over medium heat and cook, stirring constantly, until the tofu absorbs most of the liquid, 12 to 15 minutes. If the mixture begins to stick, stir in the vegetable broth, 1 tablespoon at a time, as needed.

Warm a large stainless-steel skillet over medium heat for 2 to 3 minutes. Add the avocado oil and onion and cook, stirring occasionally, until translucent and slightly brown, about 4 minutes. Add the garlic and the tofu mixture and cook, stirring often, for 5 minutes.

Add the potatoes to the skillet and cook, stirring, for 2 minutes, then cover and let simmer until the potatoes are easily pierced with a fork, 5 to 6 minutes more.

Serve the papas con chorizo with beans, vegan eggs, salsa, vegan crema, and avocado wedges and cilantro, if desired.

NOTE To make the vegan chorizo with a chewier, meatier texture, use 24 ounces firm tofu (not pre-pressed) and, before crumbling, place it in a freezer-safe container and freeze for 4 hours, or up to overnight. Thaw and then drain, pressing out any excess liquid. Repeat the freezing, thawing, and draining, then crumble the tofu and proceed as directed.

Papas Locas

———◇———

Even I can't believe a quick twenty-five-minute breakfast like this can satisfy all my cravings when it comes to Mexican food. The potatoes are perfect for meal prep—they can be refrigerated in an airtight container for up to 1 week and reheated really well in the microwave. Making these "crazy potatoes" in advance and having them on hand is a lifesaver on busy mornings when I don't have time to cook something from scratch. They're also great to pack for a lunch.

MAKES 4 TO 6 SERVINGS

2 tablespoons avocado oil

1 teaspoon cumin seeds

½ teaspoon crushed red pepper

1 medium white onion, diced

6 small to medium Yukon gold potatoes, scrubbed and roughly chopped

1 large sweet potato, scrubbed and roughly chopped

3 garlic cloves, minced

3 medium heirloom tomatoes, roughly chopped

2 large or 3 medium poblano chiles, seeded and roughly chopped

1 jalapeño chile, finely chopped

1 teaspoon fine sea salt

¼ teaspoon freshly ground black pepper

Cooked rice (see pages 39 to 43) for serving (optional)

Cooked beans (see pages 31 to 36) for serving (optional)

Corn tortillas (see page 44) or flour tortillas (see page 47) for serving (optional)

Warm a large skillet over medium heat for 2 to 3 minutes. Add the avocado oil, cumin seeds, crushed red pepper, and onion and cook, stirring often, until the onion is translucent and slightly browned, 4 to 5 minutes.

Add the all potatoes and the garlic to the skillet and cook, stirring occasionally, until the potatoes are golden brown and crispy, 5 to 6 minutes. Add the tomatoes, poblanos, jalapeño, salt, and black pepper; turn the heat to medium-low; cover; and simmer until the tomatoes are still mostly intact while the other vegetables are slightly browned and aromatic, 6 to 8 minutes. If the mixture is a bit dry, stir in water, 1 tablespoon at a time, as needed.

Serve the papas locas on its own or pair with rice, beans, and tortillas.

Chilaquiles Rojos

One morning after a fiesta, I got to sit alone with my abuelita and watch as she fried tortillas and roasted tomatoes and chiles. She said, "Mijo, estos son chilaquiles rojos," meaning "Son, these are red chilaquiles"; and since I was the first one awake, I would get the best chilaquiles, as they are best served immediately. She was right; those chilaquiles had the crispiest bite and the most flavorful sauce.

Chilaquiles is a simple dish that's easy to prepare for breakfast and often made using leftover tortillas, tomatoes, and black beans from the dinner before. It's a much-loved Mexican meal that makes everyone happy.

MAKES 4 TO 6 SERVINGS

12 corn tortillas (see page 44)

2 tablespoons avocado oil

5 medium tomatoes, roughly chopped

1 jalapeño chile, roughly chopped

½ medium white onion, roughly chopped

4 garlic cloves, roughly chopped

1 tablespoon adobo sauce from canned chipotle chiles

1 tablespoon apple cider vinegar

2 teaspoons ground cumin

Fine sea salt

¾ cup shredded vegan cheese (I like vegan mozzarella), plus more for topping

Frijoles Fritos (page 103) or Black Beans (see page 135) for topping

Sliced avocado for topping

Chopped red onion for topping

Chopped cilantro leaves and tender stems for topping

Preheat the oven to 350°F. Lightly coat two or three baking sheets with cooking spray.

Cut each tortilla into four equal wedges, arrange in a single layer on the prepared baking sheets, and then lightly coat with cooking spray. Bake until crisp, 15 to 17 minutes. Remove from the oven and set aside.

Meanwhile, in a large skillet over medium heat, warm the avocado oil. Add four-fifths of the tomatoes, the jalapeño, white onion, garlic, and adobo sauce and cook, stirring occasionally, until softened, about 15 minutes. Transfer to a high-powered blender or large food processor. Set the uncleaned skillet aside.

Add the vinegar, cumin, and 1 teaspoon salt to the vegetables in the blender and blend until smooth. Return the mixture to the skillet and simmer over medium-high heat, stirring frequently, for 5 minutes. Turn the heat to low, then taste and add more salt, if needed. Add the baked tortillas and fold gently into the sauce. Add the ¾ cup vegan cheese and simmer until the cheese is (mostly) melted, about 5 minutes.

Serve the chilaquiles topped with beans, avocado, the remaining tomato, red onion, additional cheese, and cilantro, as desired.

Chilaquiles Verdes

These chilaquiles with green sauce are more like nachos. Instead of baking it in one big dish, I fry the tortillas until crispy and then layer them with a bright tomatillo sauce and toppings directly on the serving plates. The green sauce is inspired by the native part of my culture and is slightly nutty from pepitas. I like these for breakfast, but they make a great snack for any time of the day. You can make the chips and sauce ahead of time and keep them in separate containers to assemble whenever you get a craving. Store the chips at room temperature, and the sauce in the refrigerator; each will last for up to 2 weeks if unopened.

MAKES 4 SERVINGS

1 pound tomatillos, husks removed

2 serrano chiles

3 garlic cloves

1 cup firmly packed chopped cilantro leaves and tender stems

¼ cup pepitas

2 teaspoons fresh lime juice

1 teaspoon Himalayan pink salt

4 to 5 tablespoons coconut oil, or as needed

18 corn tortillas (see page 44), cut into fourths

¼ white onion, minced

Vegan queso fresco (see page 164) for sprinkling

Frijoles Fritos (page 103) for serving

Curtido (page 174) for topping

Salsa al Horno (page 151) for topping

Bring a small pot of water to a boil over high heat. Meanwhile, wash any sticky residue off of the tomatillos.

Add the tomatillos to the pot, turn the heat to medium-high, and boil, partially covered, for 5 minutes. Add the serranos, boil for 5 minutes more, and then drain. Stem the serranos.

In a high-powered blender, combine the tomatillos, serranos, garlic, cilantro, pepitas, lime juice, and salt and blend on high speed until completely smooth, about 1 minute. Set this sauce aside.

Warm a large cast-iron skillet over high heat for 3 to 4 minutes. Turn the heat to medium-low (or medium if you have a smaller flame) and add 1 table-spoon of the coconut oil. Working in batches, cover the bottom of the skillet with tortillas—it's okay if they overlap a bit—and fry until crispy, about 3 min-utes on each side, moving them around occasionally for even frying. Add 1 table-spoon coconut oil to the skillet for each new batch.

Divide the tortilla chips among four plates, drizzle generously with the sauce, and sprinkle with the onion and vegan queso fresco. Serve with a gen-erous side of beans, topped with some curtido and salsa.

Gorditas

I actually didn't like gorditas when I was growing up. These puffy disks would often be too thick, with too little filling, and all you could taste was the masa. Now that I'm making them myself, I can control the thickness and fill them with whatever I want. Usually, it's some leftover entrée—I especially love them with Guisado de Papa y Nopales (page 96) or Hongos a la Diabla (page 88). For this recipe, I fill the gorditas with beans. They're kind of a blank canvas.

I remember waking up to the slapping sounds of my grandma making these for breakfast. I channeled her energy for this recipe, and I learned to love them.

MAKES 6 SERVINGS

MASA

2 cups Maseca Azul instant blue corn masa flour

1 teaspoon Himalayan pink salt

1¼ cups water, plus more as needed

3 tablespoons avocado oil

FILLING

1 tablespoon avocado oil

¼ white onion, finely diced

1 garlic clove, minced

Two 15-ounce cans pinto beans, drained, or 4 cups cooked beans (see page 31)

1 teaspoon Himalayan pink salt

Avocado oil for drizzling

Fermented Vegan Crema (page 163) for topping

Salsa (see pages 147 to 156) for topping

To make the masa: In a large mixing bowl, combine the masa flour and salt. Slowly add the 1¼ cups water, mixing with clean hands, until completely combined. Add the avocado oil and mix until a moist dough the consistency of soft Play-Doh forms. (You should be able to form a bit of the dough into a ball that's easily flattened with no deep cracks; some small cracks are okay). If needed, add more water, 1 teaspoon at a time, to get the right consistency. Shape the dough into one large ball, place into a bowl, and cover with plastic wrap. Set aside in the refrigerator.

To make the filling: Warm a saucepan over medium-low heat for 2 to 3 minutes. Add the avocado oil, onion, and garlic and cook, stirring often, just until the onion is translucent and lightly golden, 3 to 4 minutes. Add the beans and let simmer until almost dry, 3 to 4 minutes. Add the salt, remove from the heat, and mash the beans with a bean or potato masher or the back of a wooden spoon. Let cool to room temperature.

Remove the masa from the refrigerator and tear off a chunk about the size of a golf ball. Roll it into a ball and press it with your fingers, flattening it and forming it into a small bowl—the beans will eventually go in the depression. Pinch all around the edges to thin and extend them. Spoon about 1½ tablespoons of the filling into the center and bring the edges together and seal them. Try to form a ball enclosing the beans in the center. If needed, use pinches of additional masa to fully close and seal, but it's okay if a little filling leaks out.

Gently turn and flatten the ball between your palms, until the gordita is the size and shape of a hockey puck. Repeat with the remaining masa and filling; for six gorditas total.

Warm a large cast-iron skillet over medium heat for 2 to 3 minutes, then add a light drizzle of avocado oil. Working in batches, place the gorditas in the skillet in a single layer and fry for 3 minutes on one side. Flip and fry for 2 minutes more.

Transfer the gorditas to individual plates and serve hot, topped with fermented vegan crema and salsa.

Tortas de Tofu

———◇———

Growing up, I was often shooed out of the kitchen because my family (like most Mexican households) didn't encourage boys to cook, but one of the only times I was allowed to help was when making tortas. To make as many sandwiches as possible, my relatives would need all hands on deck for the assembly line. I was on bread prep duty; my job was to slather each crusty bolillo roll (essential for tortas!) with mayo, then pass it to the next person, who would add the chiles; it would continue down the line until the torta was complete.

I really miss such family moments. Now when I slather the bread with vegan mayo for these brunch-worthy tortas, I think back on those times. And I'm the entire assembly line! I coat the tofu slabs with seasoned flour, fry 'til crisp, and layer them in the sandwiches with the usual accompaniments: lettuce, tomato, beans, and avocado.

MAKES 4 SERVINGS

CHIPOTLE BARBECUE SAUCE

¾ cup ketchup

2 tablespoons adobo sauce from canned chipotle chiles

2 tablespoons apple cider vinegar

1 tablespoon agave nectar

1 teaspoon garlic powder

½ teaspoon soy sauce

1 pinch freshly ground black pepper

FRIED TOFU

24 ounces extra-firm pre-pressed tofu (see Note, page 20), patted dry

5 tablespoons all-purpose flour

2 tablespoons nutritional yeast

1 tablespoon cornstarch

2 teaspoons salt-free all-purpose seasoning

½ teaspoon paprika

½ teaspoon fine sea salt

¼ teaspoon chipotle powder

3 tablespoons avocado oil

4 bolillo rolls, split

Vegan mayonnaise for spreading

Frijoles Fritos (page 103) for serving

Romaine lettuce for topping

Sliced tomatoes for topping

Sliced red onions for topping

Sliced avocado for topping

To make the barbecue sauce: In a small saucepan over medium heat, stir together the ketchup, adobo sauce, vinegar, agave nectar, garlic powder, soy sauce, and black pepper and bring to a simmer. Turn the heat to medium-low and cook, stirring constantly to prevent boiling and popping, for 4 minutes. Remove from the heat and set aside.

To make the fried tofu: Slice the tofu lengthwise in fourths to create four ½-inch-thick slabs and set aside. If you prefer crispier tofu, slice them thinner.

In a medium bowl, combine the flour, nutritional yeast, cornstarch, all-purpose seasoning, paprika, salt, and chipotle powder and stir well.

CONTINUED

Warm a large nonstick skillet over medium heat for 2 to 3 minutes, then add the avocado oil. Dip the tofu slabs into the seasoned flour, completely coating all sides. Add the tofu to the skillet and fry for 4 minutes on one side, then flip and fry for 3 minutes on the other side. Remove to a plate.

Lightly toast the rolls in a toaster oven or in a dry cast-iron skillet over medium heat. Spread a generous layer of vegan mayonnaise on the split sides, then heap and spread a spoonful of the beans on each of the bottom rolls. Slather each fried tofu in the chipotle barbecue sauce and center one on each of the bottom rolls. Top with lettuce, tomato, onion, and avocado, then close the tortas and enjoy.

Plato Tipico

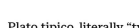

Plato tipico, literally "typical dish," is a basic plate for a Latin house. It's usually rice, beans, and a protein, plus accompaniments, like crema, plantains, and fermented toppings such as curtido. Each country has its own, using their staple foods. The version here is influenced by El Salvador and Colombia.

Whenever I take my first bite of this plato tipico, I recall all the mornings that I have devoured the dish, especially with Salvadoran crema, which is richer and creamier than the Mexican version (which is lighter and tangier because of all the lime juice). Although you could eat this at any time of the day, it's a hearty breakfast that gets you going in the morning and keeps you full.

MAKES 4 SERVINGS

BLACK BEANS
1 tablespoon avocado oil

½ cup finely diced yellow onion

1 jalapeño chile, finely diced

1 Roma tomato, finely diced

Two 15.5-ounce cans black beans; one can drained, one can undrained

½ teaspoon fine sea salt

Maduros (page 136) for serving

Cooked rice (see pages 39 to 43) for serving

Curtido (page 174) for serving

Fermented Vegan Crema (page 163) or any vegan plain yogurt for serving

Vegan queso fresco (see page 164) for serving

Sliced avocado for serving

To make the beans: Warm a small saucepan over medium heat for 2 to 3 minutes. Add the avocado oil, then the onion and jalapeño and cook, stirring often, until the onion is translucent and lightly browned, 4 to 5 minutes. Add the tomato and cook, stirring, for 3 minutes. Add all the black beans and the salt and stir together. Turn the heat to medium-low and cook for 1 minute. Using a potato masher or a fork, lightly mash the beans, then turn the heat to low and simmer until thick but still liquidy, 6 to 8 minutes. Check every 2 to 3 minutes and stir to make sure the beans don't stick to the pan.

For each plate, serve two spoonfuls of beans with some of the maduros, rice, curtido, fermented vegan crema, vegan queso fresco, and avocado.

Maduros

Mexicans love to have something sweet, like these fried (or baked) plantains, with a savory meal. Maduros aren't just one-note sweet; the caramelization gives them a great depth of flavor. You could pair this as a side for any entrée, really. Or, for a sweet treat, drizzle the plantains with my Vegan Condensed Milk (page 224).

To make maduros correctly, you need to start with plantains that are properly ripe. In this case, that means the plantains will have a nice distribution of black spots and look a bit like a yellow-and-black cow print (about 30 percent black spots over the whole plantain). If your plantains aren't ripe enough, put them in a paper bag to speed up the process. This usually takes 2 to 3 days.

MAKES 2 TO 4 SERVINGS

2 ripe plantains
1 tablespoon avocado oil

Set a medium cast-iron skillet over medium heat.

Meanwhile, cut both ends off each plantain and slice lengthwise through the skin. Run your finger through the slit to separate the peel from the plantain. Slice the plantains in half lengthwise, following the slit you already made.

Add the avocado oil to the hot skillet and use a brush or spatula to coat the entire pan. Turn the heat to medium-low, wait 1 minute, and then add all four plantain halves to the skillet. Cover and fry for 3 minutes. (Try to flip; if a plantain doesn't release easily, cook for a few minutes more or until it does.) Flip the plantains, then cook until caramelized, 3 to 4 minutes on the other side. Remove from the heat and let sit, covered, for 1½ minutes before serving.

VARIATIONS

To bake the plantains in a toaster oven, preheat the toaster oven to 350°F. Place the sliced plantains directly on the wire rack and bake for 7 minutes. Flip and bake until caramelized, about 7 minutes more. Remove from the toaster oven and let cool for 5 minutes before serving.

To bake the plantains in a conventional oven, set oven racks in the upper and lower positions and preheat to 350°F. Line a baking sheet with parchment paper or a silicone mat. Place the plantains cut-side down on the prepared baking sheet. Bake on the lower rack for 20 minutes, then transfer to the upper rack and bake until caramelized, about 10 minutes more. Remove from the oven and let cool for 5 minutes before serving.

Mushroom Menudo

Menudo is a rich soup that's typically eaten for breakfast because it's said to cure hangovers. The main ingredient is tripe, so I thought about making a plant-based version with Nebrodini Bianco mushrooms. They have a meaty texture and ripples that resemble tripe. Then I added cauliflower mushrooms because they have the mouthfeel of tripe. Both mushrooms release their juices in the soup, giving this menudo incredible depth. The flavors are on point and are very close to the traditional version. My family devoured it. They weren't hungover at the time, but I bet this soup would do the trick if they had been!

4 California chiles (see Note)

3 large garlic cloves

5 to 7 tablespoons avocado oil

1 pound Nebrodini Bianco mushrooms

1 white onion, diced

8 cups vegetable broth

1 pound cauliflower mushrooms

1 teaspoon fine sea salt

1 pinch freshly ground black pepper

Roughly chopped cilantro leaves and tender stems for topping

2 to 3 tablespoons dried oregano

Lime wedges for squeezing

Quesadillas (see pages 75 to 81), corn tortillas (see page 44), or flour tortillas (see page 47) for serving

In a small saucepan over medium-low heat, combine the chiles, garlic, and 3 tablespoons of the avocado oil and cook, stirring, until the garlic is golden, about 4 minutes; lower the heat if the garlic browns too quickly. Remove the garlic and set aside. Keep on stirring until the chiles puff up a little and the oil is golden orange, 2 to 3 minutes more. Remove the chiles and let cool, then stem. Remove the saucepan from the heat and let the chile oil cool.

In a large pot over medium heat, warm 2 tablespoons avocado oil (add the remaining 2 tablespoons oil, if a richer soup is desired).

Meanwhile, slice the Nebrodini mushrooms in half. Working in batches, if necessary, add them to the pot in a single layer without crowding. Cook, flipping only once, until seared to a golden color, about 3 minutes on each side. They should be easy to flip once properly seared. Remove from the heat and set aside.

In a high-powered blender, combine half the diced onion, 2 cups of the vegetable broth, and the reserved garlic and chiles and blend until very smooth. Strain through a fine-mesh sieve into a bowl. Add a splash more vegetable broth to the blender, swirl to release any stuck bits, then pour into the bowl through the sieve; the sieve should strain out most of the chile flakes and seeds. Pour the mixture into the pot; add the chile oil, cauliflower mushrooms, salt, black pepper, half of the remaining onion, and the remaining vegetable broth; and set over medium heat. Bring to a simmer, cover, and cook until the mushrooms are completely orange from the sauce, about 20 minutes.

Ladle the menudo into bowls and top with cilantro, oregano, and the remaining onion. Serve with lime wedges for squeezing, alongside quesadillas or tortillas.

NOTE California chiles are red with a mild heat and smoky, savory flavor. Feel free to add a spicier chile if you want more kick.

Camote y Leche

My family can definitely be relied on for a hereditary sweet tooth—even when it comes to breakfast. Caramelized sweet potatoes and milk is a favorite in the morning; and the key to making this dish is piloncillo, an unrefined sugar that has deep toffee-like flavors (but you can also use coconut sugar). Cooking sweet potatoes with piloncillo creates a caramel in the pot. This dish is best eaten freshly made and cooled down a bit so you don't burn your tongue on the caramel. Pour milk over the sweet potatoes, and you're in heaven. You could even eat this for dessert.

MAKES 6 SERVINGS

5 medium white or orange yams, scrubbed, ends trimmed, and cut into thirds

8 ounces piloncillo, or 1 cup coconut sugar

1 thumb fresh ginger, peeled

1 teaspoon pure vanilla extract

1 pinch fine sea salt

3½ cups water

Cold macadamia milk for serving

In a medium pot over medium heat, combine the yams, piloncillo, ginger, vanilla, salt, and water and bring to a simmer. Cook for 8 minutes, then lower the heat and simmer gently until the yams are soft and the liquid in the pot resembles a caramel-like sauce, 10 to 15 minutes. You can leave the ginger in or remove and discard it, if desired.

Scoop the camote into bowls, leaving most of the caramel at the bottom of the pot to cool for about 10 minutes. Pour ½ to 1 cup macadamia milk over each bowl and then top with the caramel before serving.

CHAPTER 4

Antojitos

Before we officially come to the table at mealtime, my family indulges in antojitos, or "little cravings." Antojitos might be guacamole and chips, cactus or jicama salad, and, of course, salsas—really, anything that's light and not too filling. While I love antojitos in any form, I have a particular fondness for salsa. It harkens back to all the time I spent with mi Tia Belsabet. My aunt was like a second mother, helping to raise me while my single mom was at work. I'd hop the fence every day to get to Belsabet's house next door, and inevitably she'd say, "Se me antoja una salsita," or "I'm craving a little salsa." Mi tia would never dream of having a meal without it. Even today, Belsabet immediately reaches for the bowl of salsa and dollops it on everything. I do the same—partly out of habit but mostly because a good salsa happens to be the perfect vegan sauce.

The spicy salsas, lime-drenched veggies, and refreshing salads in this chapter can start as appetizers and then linger on the table to become a topping or side for any main dish. Antojitos add a spark that's essential to the Mexican dining experience. They're not just delicious; they're a celebration of the bold textures and colors found in Mexican cuisine and culture.

Pico de Gallo

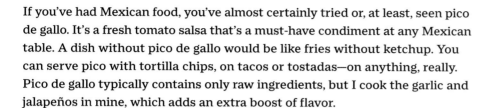

If you've had Mexican food, you've almost certainly tried or, at least, seen pico de gallo. It's a fresh tomato salsa that's a must-have condiment at any Mexican table. A dish without pico de gallo would be like fries without ketchup. You can serve pico with tortilla chips, on tacos or tostadas—on anything, really. Pico de gallo typically contains only raw ingredients, but I cook the garlic and jalapeños in mine, which adds an extra boost of flavor.

MAKES 8 TO 10 SERVINGS

Avocado oil for frying

4 garlic cloves

2 jalapeño chiles

½ red onion, cut into ¼-inch dice

5 Roma tomatoes, cut into ¼-inch dice

3 Persian cucumbers, cut into ¼-inch dice

1 cup finely chopped cilantro leaves and tender stems

¼ cup fresh lime juice

1 teaspoon fine sea salt

Set a small cast-iron skillet over medium heat. Add a drizzle of avocado oil and the garlic and jalapeños and fry, turning occasionally, until charred all over, about 6 minutes. Remove from the heat and let cool. Finely chop or mince the garlic and transfer to a large bowl. Stem and halve the jalapeños lengthwise (remove the seeds for less heat, if desired) and chop into ¼-inch dice; transfer to the bowl. Add the onion, tomatoes, cucumbers, cilantro, lime juice, and salt and mix well.

Store the pico de gallo in an airtight container in the refrigerator for up to 7 days.

Salsa Verde

According to my grandma, a good salsa verde should be very simple. It has a couple jalapeños, but they're roasted and seeded, which mellows the heat, so it's a fairly mild salsa. The tomatillos add a tartness, so using them is like squirting lemon or lime juice on a dish. This salsa goes well with a lot of foods, but especially on Taquitos de Camote (page 72); the acid punches through the richness of the fried tortillas.

MAKES 8 TO 10 SERVINGS

2 tablespoons avocado oil

6 large tomatillos, husked

2 poblano chiles, or 1 green bell pepper, stemmed and seeded

2 jalapeño chiles

½ white onion

3 garlic cloves

2 cups roughly chopped cilantro leaves and tender stems

1 teaspoon fine sea salt

In a large cast-iron skillet over medium heat, warm the avocado oil. Add the tomatillos, poblanos, jalapeños, onion, and a garlic clove in a single layer and let sear, flipping every 2 to 3 minutes. When the garlic is browned all over, about 6 minutes, transfer it to a high-powered blender.

Turn the heat to low and continue to cook the vegetables, flipping periodically, until the tomatillos soften and become yellowish green, 5 to 6 minutes more. You want the vegetables charred but not burned all the way—the char adds a smoky flavor to the salsa. Remove from the heat.

When the jalapeños are cool enough to handle, stem and remove the seeds (or keep the seeds for a spicier salsa). Transfer the jalapeños to the blender along with the contents of the skillet, the remaining two garlic cloves, cilantro, and sea salt. Blend until smooth enough to pour but still chunky enough for dipping tortilla chips, usually no more than 45 seconds. You still want a bit of texture, so avoid overblending.

Store the salsa in an airtight container in the refrigerator for up to 2 weeks. If you want it to last longer, divide into two separate containers. Finish the first container within 2 weeks; the second will last 1 week longer.

Salsa al Horno

When I want my salsa to have beautiful colors, heirloom tomatoes are my hero produce. They come in a variety of shades and complex flavors that intensify and sweeten when roasted. My mom made this salsa for our first vegan Thanksgiving. The roasted flavor complemented pretty much everything on the table, especially our No-Bake Enchiladas Verde with Jackfruit (page 51) and Chilaquiles Verdes (page 126).

MAKES 8 TO 10 SERVINGS

4 or 5 assorted large heirloom tomatoes (preferably red, yellow, and orange), halved

½ yellow onion

1 to 2 bird's eye chiles or jalapeño chiles (depending on heat preference)

4 large garlic cloves

1½ cups roughly chopped cilantro leaves and tender stems

1 tablespoon extra-virgin olive oil

1½ teaspoons fine sea salt

Preheat the oven to 400°F. Line a rimmed baking sheet with parchment paper.

Arrange the tomatoes, onion, chiles, and two of the garlic cloves on the prepared baking sheet, spacing them apart. Roast until the garlic is charred and softened, 3 to 4 minutes. Transfer the garlic to a high-powered blender.

Continue roasting the remaining vegetables until charred and softened, 8 to 10 minutes more. Remove from the oven.

When the chiles are cool enough to handle, stem and remove the seeds (if desired, for less heat). Transfer to the blender along with the other roasted vegetables and blend for 30 seconds. Add the remaining two garlic cloves, cilantro, olive oil, and sea salt and blend until well combined but still a little chunky, about 30 seconds.

Store the salsa in an airtight container in the refrigerator for up to 2 weeks. If you want it to last longer, divide into two separate containers. Finish the first container within 2 weeks; the second will last 1 week longer.

Mango Salsa

My mango salsa is about to hit the block with a full burst of flavor. Serve this bright salsa with chips or as a topping for any main course in this book. One of the reasons I called this chapter "Little Cravings" is because of this salsa; it satisfies anytime you don't want to commit to a full meal.

MAKES 6 TO 8 SERVINGS

2 tablespoons avocado oil
4 Roma tomatoes
¼ large mango, peeled
½ white onion
1 serrano chile, stemmed
2 large garlic cloves
1 teaspoon fine sea salt

In a large cast-iron skillet over medium heat, warm the avocado oil. Add the tomatoes, mango, onion, serrano, and garlic in a single layer and let sear, flipping every 2 to 3 minutes. When the garlic is browned all over, about 6 minutes, transfer it to a high-powered blender.

Turn the heat to low and continue to cook the remaining vegetables, flipping periodically, 5 to 6 minutes more. You want the vegetables charred but not burned all the way. The char adds a smoky flavor to the salsa.

Transfer the contents of the skillet to the blender, add the salt, and blend until smooth enough to pour but still chunky enough for dipping tortilla chips, usually no more than 30 seconds.

Store the salsa in an airtight container in the refrigerator for up to 2 weeks. If you want it to last longer, divide into two separate containers. Finish the first container within 2 weeks; the second will last 1 week longer.

Avocado Salsa

The next best thing to guacamole is avocado salsa. Not that this salsa is a consolation prize, by any means. You get all the creaminess from the avocado, plus tanginess from tomatillos, and a bit of smoke from the charred vegetables—the combo just hits the spot. My mother believes that avocado pits protect the salsa from browning quickly, so she drops them into the serving bowl. I don't know if the science checks out, but I'm not about to stray from this particular tradition. I secretly think that's why this salsa has such an amazing flavor.

**MAKES 8 TO
10 SERVINGS**

2 tablespoons avocado oil

4 medium tomatillos, husked

3 jalapeño chiles

½ white onion

2 large ripe avocados

3 garlic cloves

¼ cup chopped cilantro leaves and tender stems

⅓ cup water

Juice of 1 lime

1 teaspoon fine sea salt

In a large cast-iron skillet over medium heat, warm the avocado oil. Add the tomatillos, jalapeños, and onion in a single layer and let sear, flipping every 2 to 3 minutes, for 6 minutes. Turn the heat to low and continue to cook, flipping periodically, 5 to 6 minutes more. You want the vegetables charred but not burned all the way. The char adds a smoky flavor to the salsa. Remove from the heat.

When the chiles are cool enough to handle, stem and remove the seeds (if desired, for less heat). Meanwhile, halve, pit, and peel the avocados; reserve the pits for storing, if desired.

In a high-powered blender, combine the contents of the skillet, avocados, garlic, cilantro, water, lime juice, and sea salt and blend until smooth enough to pour but still chunky enough for dipping tortilla chips, usually no more than 30 seconds. (You still want a bit of texture, so avoid overblending—according to my mother, overblending will "cut" the flavor.) Transfer to a bowl and add the reserved avocado pits (if you agree with my mother that it prevents browning).

Store the salsa, covered, in the refrigerator for up to 1 week. If you want it to last longer, divide into two separate airtight containers (adding an avocado pit to each). Finish the first container within 1 week; the second will last up to 4 days longer.

Aji

———◇———

When you look at the basic ingredients for aji, you'll wonder if it's a dupe of pico de gallo (see page 147). But the ingredients are very finely chopped, so you definitely get a different texture; and somehow it tastes very different from pico de gallo. The goal for aji is to have all the components as small and uniform as possible. There's plenty of lime juice to mellow out any heat from the jalapeño, so the resulting condiment is actually great for those who don't like things too spicy. Aji is a must for Colombian Empanadas (page 52) or other savory empanadas, like lentil-cauliflower (see page 56) or mushroom-spinach (see page 59), and excellent with tacos or anything with tortillas.

**MAKES ABOUT
3 CUPS**

1 large yellow onion,
very finely chopped

2 Roma tomatoes,
very finely chopped

1 bunch cilantro,
very finely chopped

Juice of 5 limes

1 jalapeño chile, minced

2 garlic cloves, minced

1 teaspoon Himalayan
pink salt

In a medium bowl, combine the onion, tomatoes, cilantro, lime juice, jalapeño, garlic, and salt. Toss together well.

Store the aji in an airtight container in the refrigerator for up to 1 week.

Vegan Cilantro Crema

Crema is like sour cream's thinner, Latin cousin. Typically, it's made with buttermilk and heavy cream, and gets a pleasant tang from lime juice. It cools the heat of chiles and rounds out the sharp flavors in a dish. I make this easy plant-based version with cashews, which are among the creamiest of nuts. They make this crema indulgent and so irresistible, especially if you miss having dairy. Drizzle it on tacos, burritos, soups, or anywhere you want a touch of creamy richness.

**MAKES ABOUT
2 CUPS**

¾ cup raw cashew pieces, soaked in water to cover overnight (or boiled for 15 minutes)

½ cup chopped cilantro leaves and tender stems

¼ cup fresh lime juice

1 tablespoon apple cider vinegar

2 teaspoons granulated garlic

½ cup plus 2 tablespoons water

Fine sea salt

Drain the cashews and rinse with cold, fresh water.

In a high-powered blender, combine the cashews, cilantro, lime juice, vinegar, granulated garlic, and ½ cup plus 2 table-spoons water; season with salt; and blend on high speed until the blender is a bit warm to the touch and the crema is completely emulsified, 2 to 3 minutes.

Store the crema in an airtight container in the refrigerator for up to 1 week.

Vegan Chipotle Crema

Like the Vegan Cilantro Crema on page 159, you can drizzle this condiment on tacos, burritos, soups, or any dish that would welcome a creamy component. The chipotles give the crema a rich, smoky flavor. I love to serve this on green dishes, such as enchiladas verde (see page 51), or any of the taco recipes that don't already have chipotle.

**MAKES ABOUT
2½ CUPS**

1 red, orange, or yellow bell pepper

1 cup raw cashews, soaked in water to cover overnight (or boiled for 15 minutes)

¼ to ⅓ cup chipotle chiles in adobo sauce (depending on heat preference; see Note)

1½ cups vegetable broth

1 tablespoon granulated garlic

2 teaspoons smoked paprika

1 teaspoon ground cumin

½ teaspoon fine sea salt

Warm a cast-iron skillet over medium heat for 2 to 3 minutes. Place the bell pepper directly in the dry skillet and cook, turning, until charred lightly all over, about 2 minutes per side. Let cool, then, using your hands, remove the skin. Halve the bell pepper and remove and discard the seeds.

Drain the cashews and rinse with cold, fresh water.

In a high-powered blender, combine the cashews, bell pepper, chipotle chiles in adobo sauce, vegetable broth, granulated garlic, paprika, cumin, and salt and blend on high speed until the blender is a bit warm to the touch and the crema is completely emulsified, 2 to 3 minutes.

Store the crema in an airtight container in the refrigerator for up to 1 week.

NOTE Instead of the canned chipotle chiles in adobo sauce, you can substitute one dried chipotle chile, soaked overnight in ⅓ cup water. Boil until softened, about 5 minutes, then stem and reserve the cooking liquid. Add fresh water to the reserved cooking liquid to yield ½ cup liquid in total.

Fermented Vegan Crema

The previous two crema recipes in this chapter mimic the creaminess of Mexican crema. This one nails the drizzly texture. It's fermented with vegan yogurt and takes about a day (of mostly letting things sit) to make, but the payoff is so worth it. You can truly taste the tanginess. So if you're ambitious and want to get the flavor right, give this recipe a try. Once you make a batch, it can become a mother for subsequent batches. Because it's fermented, this crema will last a while in the fridge. I put it on everything, but it's especially good with Plato Tipico (page 135).

MAKES ABOUT 2 CUPS

1½ cups raw cashew pieces, soaked in water to cover overnight (or boiled for 15 minutes)

1 cup water

2 tablespoons plain vegan yogurt

2 tablespoons fresh lemon juice

¼ teaspoon fine sea salt

Drain the cashews and rinse with cold, fresh water.

In a high-powered blender, combine the cashews, 1 cup water, yogurt, lemon juice, and salt and blend on the highest setting until completely emulsified and smooth, with no grains of the nuts remaining, about 1 minute.

Transfer to a glass container, cover partially, and let sit near your oven all day. (At least 8 hours. It's best to do this on a day when you're already baking or cooking on the stove, as the ambient heat will help the crema ferment. If you aren't cooking that day, the top of the fridge is a place that sometimes generates low-level ambient heat. But make sure to push the container away from the door so you don't accidentally drop it when you open the fridge!) The crema is ready when thickened and fluffed up to about 25 percent more than the original volume.

Store the crema in an airtight container in the refrigerator for up to 2 weeks.

Vegan Queso Fresco

—◇—

Many of the recipes throughout this book call for vegan queso fresco as a topping, so you'll probably want to bookmark this page. The other option is to use store-bought queso fresco, but I guarantee that it won't be better than this recipe. This is the easiest vegan cheese recipe you can ever make. I streamlined it to remove unnecessary steps without compromising the results. The only equipment you need is your own two hands. Queso fresco is super-common in taquitos and tamales as well as sprinkled on beans. The flavor is mild and the texture is crumbly, similar to feta. In fact, you could use queso fresco in anything where you'd add feta, like a beet salad. It's also the creamy base for my Mexican Potato Salad (page 178). Along with tortillas, salsa, and crema, queso fresco is a must-have on the Mexican table.

**MAKES ABOUT
2 CUPS**

One 16-ounce package pre-pressed extra-firm tofu (see Note, page 20)

3 tablespoons vegan butter, at room temperature

2 tablespoons nutritional yeast (omit, to keep the tofu white, if desired)

1 tablespoon granulated garlic (see Note, page 60)

2 tablespoons apple cider vinegar

2 tablespoons fresh lemon juice

½ teaspoon fine sea salt

In a medium bowl, use your hands to break up the tofu just until crumbly, like feta. Add the vegan butter, nutritional yeast, granulated garlic, vinegar, lemon juice, and salt and mix well with your hands. Pack into a square or round airtight container and refrigerate for at least 2 hours or up to 2 weeks.

Invert the queso fresco onto a plate when ready to use.

Mi Tia Evelia's Ceviche de Coliflor

Every time I smell the aroma of lime and red onion, I have a Pavlovian response: I immediately start craving ceviche. To me, ceviche is less about seafood and more about the bright, fresh flavors in the marinade. In a typical ceviche, the acid in lime juice "cooks" the seafood. In my Aunt Evelia's vegan version, the acid "cooks" the cauliflower in the same way, making it luxuriously tender—all the better for soaking up the vibrant flavors in the bowl.

MAKES 8 TO 10 SERVINGS

Fine sea salt

1 large head cauliflower, tough leaves trimmed

1½ cups rainbow cherry tomatoes, cut in half, or 2 large tomatoes, diced

½ cup finely chopped cilantro leaves and tender stems

1 large red onion, finely chopped

3 garlic cloves, minced

½ cup fresh lime juice, plus up to 2 tablespoons (optional)

2 tablespoons apple cider vinegar

2 tablespoons extra-virgin olive oil

½ teaspoon freshly ground black pepper

Diced avocado for topping (optional)

Tortilla chips or tostadas for serving

Fill a large bowl with ice and water; set aside.

In a large pot, combine 4 cups water with a pinch of salt and bring to a boil. Add the cauliflower and boil until slightly tender but not mushy, 6 to 7 minutes. Drain the cauliflower and submerge in the bowl of ice water until completely cool, 3 to 4 minutes. Drain again and then chop into small, bite-size florets. Transfer to a large bowl.

Add the tomatoes, cilantro, onion, and garlic to the bowl and gently mix together. Pour in the lime juice, vinegar, and olive oil. Add 1 teaspoon salt and the pepper and mix well.

Let the ceviche sit for 1 hour at room temperature or in the refrigerator overnight. The longer it marinates, the more tender and flavorful it becomes.

Serve the ceviche topped with diced avocado (if desired) and with tortilla chips or tostadas.

Coconut Aguachile

——◇——

You may look at ceviche and aguachile and wonder, "They're both seafood marinated in lime juice, so what's the difference?" Aguachile is like that friend who's always *extra*. As the name suggests, it marinates in a mixture of chiles blended with water, so aguachile is spicier than ceviche (which may or may not have chiles). I got the idea for this recipe when I was digging out the flesh of a young coconut at a Thai restaurant. Coconut flesh has a succulent texture that's similar to fish and can likewise soak up flavors. It also has a richness that makes it as satisfying as shrimp or scallops. I knew this dish was a winner when my mom and aunts all gave it a thumbs-up—although they thought it could use more spice, which even I can't handle!

MAKES 6 TO 8 SERVINGS

3 to 4 young Thai coconuts (to yield about 3 cups coconut flesh)

1 red onion, thinly sliced on a mandoline

Juice of 2 limes

2 large Persian cucumbers, cut into 1 by ¼-inch strips

1 recipe Aguachile Sauce (page 173)

Tortilla chips or tostadas for serving

Vegan mayonnaise, sliced avocado, chopped cilantro, and freshly ground black pepper for serving

Using a knife, trim the top of one coconut; the outer husk should come off easily to expose the coconut shell. Using a cleaver, gently tap the shell to create an opening and then remove the shell. Strain the coconut water through a fine-mesh sieve into a bowl; reserve and refrigerate ¼ cup of the coconut water (for the aguachile sauce) and save the rest for another use (or just drink it). Discard any shavings in the sieve. Using the back of a spoon, gently scrape out the coconut flesh, following the contour inside the shell; you should be able to remove all the flesh in one go. Set the flesh aside. Repeat with the remaining coconuts.

Cut the coconut flesh into 1 by ¼-inch strips and transfer to an airtight container. Add the red onion and lime juice, stir until well combined, and then refrigerate for at least 2 hours, or preferably overnight for best results.

In a large bowl, combine the lime-cooked coconut, the cucumbers, and aguachile sauce and mix well. (At this point, you can transfer to an airtight container and refrigerate for up to 1 week.)

Serve the coconut aguachile with tortilla chips. Or spread vegan mayonnaise on tostadas and top with the aguachile, avocado, a bit of cilantro, and pepper.

Aguachile Sauce

With lime juice, fresh coconut water, and two kinds of chiles, this sauce is bursting with flavor. There's a bit of heat from the serranos and jalapeño, but just enough to make it thrilling. My spice tolerance isn't as high as my family's. My aunt has the highest tolerance at a level 10, my mother is at 6, and I used to be at a piddly level 2. Ha! Ha! I would always be sweating and burning up my lips when I had spicy food. When I first saw my tia make her aguachile sauce, I was astonished at how many chiles she added—she used three times the amount I do! When I tried the sauce, I got a rush of blood to my head! I was spiced up and laughing from the pain. But after marinating, the sauce mellowed out a lot. Well, you don't have to worry about being in pain from this recipe. Even my partner enjoys this dish, and he really can't tolerate any heat. Of course, if you like it spicy, don't let me stop you from adding more chiles.

MAKES ABOUT 2 CUPS

3 cups chopped cilantro leaves and tender stems

2 serrano chiles, stemmed

1 jalapeño chile, stemmed

¼ white onion

3 garlic cloves

½ cup fresh lime juice

2 teaspoons fine sea salt

¼ cup fresh coconut water (see page 170)

In a high-powered blender, combine the cilantro, serranos, jalapeño, onion, garlic, lime juice, salt, and coconut water and blend until smooth, about 90 seconds.

Store the sauce in an airtight container in the refrigerator for up to 5 days.

Curtido

I have a weird food confession: I used to put sauerkraut on tacos. Now hear me out, sauerkraut has a sour funk that actually goes well with Mexican food. So when I first tried this fermented cabbage from my Salvadoran neighbors, I immediately loved it. It's like Latin sauerkraut; but unlike its German counterpart, this one pickles very quickly. Curtido is the essential condiment for pupusas (thick Salvadoran stuffed flatbreads), but I still like it on tacos, and with anything savory.

MAKES 2 QUARTS

½ green cabbage, thinly sliced on a mandoline or with a knife

1½ cups shredded carrots

¼ cup apple cider vinegar

2 tablespoons dried oregano

1½ teaspoons fine sea salt

In a large saucepan, bring 5 cups water to a boil. Meanwhile, place the cabbage in a heatproof colander in the sink. Pour the boiling water over the cabbage and let drain. Rinse with cold water until the cabbage is cool, then drain again.

Transfer the cabbage to a large bowl. Add the carrots, vinegar, oregano, and salt and mix well. Divide between two 1-quart jars, leaving space at the top for the resulting gases, and close the lids. Let ferment at room temperature for 24 hours, then refrigerate for 2 days before eating.

Store the curtido in the refrigerator for up to 2 months after opening.

Ensalada de Nopales

If you've never had nopales (prickly pear cactus pads), you're in for a treat. The flavor is slightly tangy and herbaceous, almost reminiscent of a cucumber. I combine them with sharp and pungent ingredients here to make a bright, refreshing salad. You can find nopales at Latin markets, often already cooked and sliced. That will save you the hassle of shaving off the thorns, which are actually the leaves of the cactus. I include directions for this whole process because when I was growing up in El Barrio, I used to harvest nopales from our neighbors' houses—with permission, of course! Almost everybody had nopales growing in their yard, so much so they'd put them out in boxes, practically begging passersby to take them off their hands. If you live in a climate where nopales grow, maybe you can get them straight from the source!

MAKES 6 TO 8 SERVINGS

About 1 pound nopales, or 3 cups cooked, sliced nopales (see Note, page 96)

¼ white onion

1 garlic clove

Fine sea salt

3 large heirloom tomatoes, cut into ½-inch dice

1 cup chopped cilantro leaves and tender stems

1 red onion, cut into ½-inch dice

3 tablespoons fresh lime juice

Bring a medium pot of water to a boil. There should be enough water to cover the nopales.

Meanwhile, trim off the sides and thorns from the nopales, if necessary, running a sharp knife back and forth over the surface until completely clean. Cut the nopales lengthwise into strips, then cut crosswise into bite-size strips. Transfer to the boiling water. Add the white onion, garlic, and ½ teaspoon salt and boil, watching closely, until the nopales are tender, about 10 minutes. (The nopales will exude a sticky fluid [similar to okra] and may foam up. If this happens, lower the heat and add a little vegetable oil to prevent overflowing the pot.) Drain in a fine-mesh sieve and rinse with cold water; discard the onion and garlic. Set aside in the sieve to continue to drain.

Meanwhile, in a large bowl, combine the tomatoes, cilantro, red onion, and lime juice. Add the cooked nopales, mix well, and stir in 1 teaspoon salt.

Serve the salad right away or store in an airtight container in the refrigerator for up to 10 days.

TIP *My grandma always saves the nopales cooking water and drinks it hot, like a tea, sweetened with some piloncillo, an unrefined whole cane sugar. The enzymes from the nopales are believed to aid with digestion. I prefer to drink the tea chilled; but either way, give it a try!*

Mexican Potato Salad

My memories of potato salad are inextricably linked to my aunt, who often served it with burgers and other American food. Hers included ingredients that appeal to the Mexican palate: charred poblano chiles, corn, and garlic. While she would bind her potato salad with mayo, I make mine with vegan queso fresco and a little vegan butter (or you can swap in vegan mayo). Creamy, without feeling too heavy, this dish is a great side at barbecues, picnics, and potlucks.

MAKES 8 SERVINGS

9 large yellow potatoes, such as Yukon gold, scrubbed but not peeled

Fine sea salt

3 poblano chiles

1 cup vegan queso fresco (see page 164) or vegan cream cheese

1 cup thinly sliced green onions

One 16-ounce can no-salt-added sweet corn, drained

3 tablespoons vegan butter

2 garlic cloves

1 teaspoon freshly ground black pepper

Place the potatoes and a pinch of salt in a large pot and add enough water to cover by 2 inches. Bring to a boil and cook until the potatoes can be pierced with a fork, 15 to 20 minutes.

Meanwhile, place each poblano directly over the flame on the stove (or on a rimmed baking sheet under the broiler) and cook, turning occasionally with tongs, until charred all over, about 5 minutes for each. Set aside and let cool.

Fill a large bowl with ice and water.

When the potatoes are tender, drain and then submerge them in the bowl of ice water until cool, about 4 minutes. Drain again and transfer to another large bowl. (You can peel them, if you like, but I keep the skins on.) Using a potato masher, mash the potatoes, leaving some bigger chunks.

Holding the poblanos under running water, remove the charred skin with your fingers. Pat dry, stem and seed them, and then cut into bite-size strips or squares. Add them to the potatoes along with the vegan queso fresco, green onions, corn, vegan butter, garlic, black pepper, and 1 teaspoon salt and mix well.

Serve the potato salad right away or store in an airtight container in the refrigerator for up to 1 week.

CHAPTER 5

Bebidas

—◇—

When I was a kid, I wasn't allowed to drink soda; but I always had access to homemade jugos, or juices, in our refrigerator. We never bought juice at the store, not only because it was too expensive but because nothing store-bought could compare to mi mama's traditional juices made from tamarind, watermelon, hibiscus, or papaya.

All over Latin America and in El Barrio, the neighborhood I grew up in, you'll see street vendors selling fresh juices. Whenever there was a fiesta in my neighborhood, glass pitchers filled with colorful juices would line the tables like floral arrangements. These traditional beverages are refreshing on a hot day, but they also pair perfectly with the rich and sometimes spicy flavors in Mexican food.

As an adult, I still drink homemade juice regularly, but my tastes have changed. I love the traditional flavors of Mexican juices, but usually without the added sugar. Occasionally, I might add a little honey or coconut sugar to sweeten things, and I often add vegetables and healing spices that help fight inflammation. While I still love a glass of cold jugo (my fave is celery, ginger, and fennel) on a hot summer afternoon, I'm more likely to blend fruit and vegetables into a healthful glass of juice that I'll drink for breakfast or to support intermittent fasting.

Because I believe in a balanced lifestyle, I sometimes like to enjoy an alcoholic beverage with my meals; and in my family, it is definitely tradition to serve cocktails. After all, sometimes a celebration just demands a round of margaritas! All of the bebida recipes that follow are delicious and satisfying drinks with or without the addition of alcohol. When one of them could make for an excellent cocktail, I've included a recipe to utilize the component in un cóctel.

The thirst-quenching bebidas in this chapter show how traditional recipes can be changed in simple ways to fit into a healthier lifestyle.

Malteada de Papaya

This recipe is based on the breakfast smoothie my mom used to make for me when I was younger. She would even include the papaya seeds, saying they're super-good for me—and they are! (But you can leave them out if you want to avoid them.) I didn't like papaya on its own, but I loved it in this smoothie.

My mom was always working back then and never seemed to be around, but I remember she would say, "Bye, hijo" and hand me this smoothie. So, in a way, having that smoothie reminded me of her love even when she couldn't be there in person.

MAKES 6 SERVINGS

3 cups roughly chopped ripe peeled papaya (see Note; seeded, if desired)

2 cups roughly chopped peeled pineapple

1 banana, peeled

1½ cups water (or unsweetened plant-based milk, for a creamier smoothie)

Spritz of lime juice, plus lime wedges for garnish (optional)

1 pinch fine sea salt

In a high-powered blender, combine the papaya, pineapple, banana, water, lime juice, and salt and blend on high speed until completely smooth, 30 to 45 seconds.

Store the smoothie in an airtight container in the refrigerator for up to 1 week. When ready to serve, pour into individual glasses and garnish each with a lime wedge, if desired.

NOTE To make sure your papaya is truly sweet, seek out one with a peel that looks a little moldy—the flesh inside will be fine!

Oat Milk Horchata

My Tia Chely was wise to oat milk long before it started showing up in hipster coffee shops and gourmet markets. I still remember watching her blend homemade oat milk in her kitchen, surrounded by the heady aroma of cinnamon. Mexican horchata is usually made from rice, but my aunt was trying to sneak more healthful options into my uncle's diet; and she knew that oats provided nutrients such as manganese, phosphorus, copper, iron, magnesium, and fiber. Aunt Chely's oat milk horchata is truly delicious and inspired my version here, which is sweetened with dates instead of white sugar.

MAKES 6 TO 8 SERVINGS

4 quarts water

1 cinnamon stick, plus more for garnish (optional)

1 cup rolled oats (see Note)

1 cup Vegan Condensed Milk (page 224)

½ cup pitted dates, soaked in water to cover overnight and then drained, or ¼ cup cane sugar

In a medium saucepan over high heat, bring 1 quart of the water to a boil. Add the cinnamon stick and boil for 20 minutes. Then remove and discard the cinnamon stick and set aside the cinnamon water to cool completely (or transfer to a freezer-safe container and freeze for 25 minutes).

Meanwhile, in a high-powered blender, combine the remaining 3 quarts water, the oats, vegan condensed milk, and dates and blend on high speed until smooth, 45 to 60 seconds. Strain through a fine-mesh sieve (or cheesecloth-lined sieve) into a large bowl or pitcher, then add the cooled cinnamon water and stir well.

Store the horchata in an airtight container in the refrigerator for up to 1 week. When ready to serve, pour into individual glasses and garnish each with a cinnamon stick, if desired.

NOTE You could substitute 2 cups white rice for the oats, if desired.

Jugo de Apio y Manzana

Once again, my mom was ahead of the game when it came to juicing. She was into making her own juices before it became a "thing." She didn't even own a juicer. She just whizzed up the ingredients in a blender. This juice has an entire bunch of celery, but you'd never know from the tart green apple flavor here.

MAKES 4 TO 6 SERVINGS

5 Granny Smith apples, peeled, cored, and roughly chopped

½ cup pitted dates, soaked in water overnight and then drained, or ¼ cup cane sugar

1 large bunch celery, roughly chopped, plus celery stalks for garnish (optional)

4 cups water

Juice of 2 limes

In a high-powered blender, combine the apples and dates and blend on high speed until smooth, 45 to 60 seconds. Strain through a nut milk bag (or cheesecloth-lined sieve), squeezing the juice into a large bowl or pitcher.

Add the celery and 2 cups of the water to the blender and blend on medium speed for 45 seconds. Strain into the large bowl or pitcher; discard the fibers. Add the lime juice and remaining 2 cups water and stir together.

Store the juice in an airtight container in the refrigerator for up to 1 week. When ready to serve, pour into individual glasses and garnish each with a celery stalk, if desired.

Jugo de Espinaca y Piña

According to my mom, this pineapple-spinach juice recipe has been in our family for years. You can drink it chilled. You can also buy frozen versions of it in a bag in Michoacán. So if you want, freeze any excess for up to 1 month and use it to make raspado, which is shaved ice. If you pick a good, ripe pineapple (see Tip), it'll provide the sweetness to make this taste like a treat, in either liquid or frozen form.

MAKES 4 TO 6 SERVINGS

1 ripe pineapple, peeled, cored, and roughly chopped, plus pineapple cubes for garnish (optional)

6 cups water

5 ounces spinach

Juice of 1 lemon

¼ to ⅓ cup cane sugar (depending on the sweetness of the pineapple)

In a high-powered blender, combine the pineapple, water, spinach, and lemon juice and blend on high speed until smooth, 45 to 60 seconds. Strain through a nut milk bag (or cheesecloth-lined sieve), squeezing the juice into a large bowl or pitcher; discard the fibers. Taste and add the sugar, if needed, and stir well.

Store the juice in an airtight container in the refrigerator for up to 4 days. When ready to serve, pour into individual glasses and garnish each with a few skewered pineapple cubes, if desired.

TIP *To choose a ripe pineapple, look for one that's more yellow than green but still firm. The leaves should look a bit dry and wilted. Sniff the bottom; it should smell kind of overripe and alcoholic.*

Jugo de Canela y Naranja

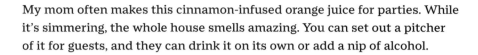

My mom often makes this cinnamon-infused orange juice for parties. While it's simmering, the whole house smells amazing. You can set out a pitcher of it for guests, and they can drink it on its own or add a nip of alcohol.

MAKES 4 TO 6 SERVINGS

3 cups water

3 cinnamon sticks

4½ cups fresh navel oranges juice, plus orange twists for garnish (optional)

¼ cup fresh lime juice

In a small saucepan over medium heat, combine the water and cinnamon sticks and bring to a boil. Turn the heat to low and simmer for 20 minutes. Then remove from the heat and let cool. Remove and discard the cinnamon sticks. Stir the orange juice and lime juice into the cinnamon water.

Store the juice in an airtight container in the refrigerator for up to 1 week. When ready to serve, pour into individual glasses and garnish each with an orange twist, if desired.

TIP *Boil additional cinnamon sticks and use the cinnamon water to clean your kitchen, including wood. It works because cinnamon is a disinfectant. I learned about this when I went to South America and wondered why the shops smelled so good. The lady explained that she cleaned the floors with cinnamon water.*

Pepino y Limón Agua Fresca

—◇—

Cucumber and lime are traditional ingredients for agua fresca. In Mexico, you can get the drink frozen in a bag and either eat it as is or drink it after it melts. It's unbelievably refreshing. This was a flavor that we always had at parties. My mom prided herself in making hers from scratch instead of buying soda.

MAKES 6 SERVINGS

3 large Persian cucumbers, peeled if the skin is waxy, cut into ½-inch-thick half-moons

¾ cup fresh lime juice

⅓ cup agave nectar, plus 2 tablespoons

6 cups water

Ice cubes for serving

In a high-powered blender, combine the cucumbers, lime juice, and ⅓ cup agave nectar and blend on high speed until smooth, about 30 seconds. Strain through a nut milk bag (or cheesecloth-lined sieve), squeezing the juice into a large bowl or pitcher; discard the fibers. (Reserve 1 cup for the Para los Agrios on page 213, if desired). Stir in the water and remaining 2 tablespoons agave nectar.

Store the agua fresca in an airtight container in the refrigerator for up to 4 days. Serve over ice.

Jengibre y Limón Agua Fresca

Mi mama said this ginger lemonade was a must in my cookbook. One day, she was really sick and couldn't go to work. I decided to stay home to help her get better. All day, I tried to get her to eat some ginger or drink ginger tea. I told her about ginger's healing and immune-boosting properties, and that it would help her sore throat. No luck. She kept telling me she didn't like the spicy zing of ginger. Finally, I decided to make lemonade with ginger juice, and using some coconut nectar to mask the spiciness of the ginger. What do you know? Mi mama loved it, and she felt better!

Now, she makes my ginger lemonade for every fiesta. When I overhear her telling everyone how healthful it is, it puts a huge smile on my face.

MAKES 10 SERVINGS

5½ cups water

3 large thumbs ginger, unpeeled

¾ cup fresh lemon juice, plus lemon slices for garnish

⅓ cup coconut nectar or agave nectar

Ice cubes for serving

10 small oregano sprigs

In a high-powered blender, combine 1 cup of the water and the ginger and blend on high speed until smooth, 45 to 60 seconds. Strain through a fine-mesh sieve into a large pitcher; discard the solids. Add the remaining 4½ cups water, the lemon juice, and coconut nectar and stir well.

Store the agua fresca in an airtight container in the refrigerator for up to 7 days. Serve over ice, garnished with the oregano sprigs and lemon slices.

Albahaca y Limón Agua Fresca

The basil in this lemonade puts a floral, fresh spin on a classic cooling drink. It goes really well with the Meyer lemon juice. Meyer lemons are abundant throughout the year in the San Francisco Bay Area; but if you're somewhere else, try to get your hands on them. Their juice has a more nuanced citrus flavor than regular lemon juice. It's great on its own, but the real kicker is adding tequila or vodka to the drink.

**MAKES 4 TO
6 SERVINGS**

4 cups water

1 cup fresh Meyer lemon juice

¼ cup cane sugar

1 pinch fine sea salt

1 bunch basil

Ice cubes for serving

In a large pitcher, combine the water, lemon juice, sugar, and salt and stir well. Add the basil and let infuse for 20 minutes before serving over ice.

Store the agua fresca in an airtight container in the refrigerator for up to 10 days (but remove the basil after the third day because it will turn brown).

Agua Fresca de Piña

This pineapple agua fresca is the ultimate hot-weather refresher. The little kick from jalapeño warms you up and then cools you down.

MAKES 6 SERVINGS

4 cups 1-inch pineapple cubes

½ jalapeño chile

½ cup fresh lime juice

¼ cup agave nectar

3 cups water

Ice cubes for serving

In a high-powered blender, combine the pineapple, jalapeño, lime juice, and agave nectar and blend on high speed until smooth, about 45 seconds. Strain through a nut milk bag (or cheesecloth-lined sieve), squeezing the juice into a large bowl or pitcher; discard the fibers. Stir in the water.

Store the agua fresca in an airtight container in the refrigerator for up to 7 days. Serve over ice.

Agua Fresca de Tamarindo

—◇—

This is the agua fresca that we have at every gathering. It's uniquely sweet and sour, and goes so well with food. Usually, more than one person brings a batch; and it's almost like a competition—my mom says hers is the best, and I have to agree! This recipe is based on her method and is pretty traditional.

Peeling and seeding the tamarind is a little tedious, but don't even think about taking a shortcut with packaged tamarind pulp. The result won't be the same, and it definitely won't win the party.

MAKES 4 OR 5 SERVINGS

One 1.2-pound package tamarind in shells
8 cups water
¼ cup agave nectar
Ice cubes for serving

Carefully remove and discard the hard, thin outer shells from the tamarind, along with any fibers stuck to the pulp inside. Place the pulp in a large jar or container and add enough of the water to cover, about 3 cups. Let soak overnight.

Strain the tamarind in a fine-mesh sieve over a large bowl, reserving the liquid in the bowl. Working with one tamarind at a time, squeeze and discard the seeds from the pulp; drop the pulp into the liquid in the bowl.

Transfer ½ cup of the tamarind pulp and liquid to a high-powered blender. (Reserve the remaining tamarind pulp and liquid for another batch.) Blend on high speed until smooth with some large chunks, about 15 seconds. Add 1 cup water, turn the speed to low, and blend until just combined, about 15 seconds more. Strain through the sieve into a large pitcher, add the agave nectar and remaining 4 cups water, and stir.

Store the agua fresca in an airtight container in the refrigerator for up to 7 days. Serve over ice.

VARIATION

If you don't have time to soak the tamarind overnight, place the pulp in a medium saucepan and add enough of the water to cover, about 3 cups. Set over medium heat, bring to a boil, cover partially, and continue to boil until the liquid becomes thick, about 15 minutes. Remove from the heat and let cool for 30 minutes. This method yields a more-concentrated liquid, so you'll need only ¼ cup tamarind pulp and liquid for the agua fresca.

Agua Fresca de Hibiscus

Not to be morbid, but my mom always used to tell me that hibiscus is the color of blood, and therefore this agua fresca is good for your blood. I thought she was making it up but it's actually true! I confirmed it with scholarly articles, which say that hibiscus may help lower blood pressure. Maybe that's why I always feel better after having this tart, crimson-colored drink.

MAKES 8 SERVINGS

1½ cups dried
hibiscus flowers

11 cups water

⅓ cup agave nectar

Rinse the hibiscus flowers under running water for 2 minutes to clean them.

In a medium pot over high heat, combine the hibiscus and 3 cups of the water and bring to a boil. Turn the heat to medium, cover partially, and boil for 20 minutes. Strain through a fine-mesh sieve into a large pot, then pour the remaining 8 cups water through the sieve with the hibiscus. (You can discard the hibiscus or save it for garnish or to nibble on later.) Add the agave nectar, stir together, and then let cool.

Store the agua fresca in an airtight container in the refrigerator for up to 1 week. When ready to serve, pour into individual glasses and garnish each with a reserved hibiscus flower, if desired.

Ponche

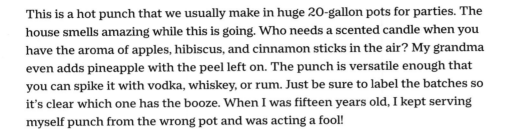

This is a hot punch that we usually make in huge 20-gallon pots for parties. The house smells amazing while this is going. Who needs a scented candle when you have the aroma of apples, hibiscus, and cinnamon sticks in the air? My grandma even adds pineapple with the peel left on. The punch is versatile enough that you can spike it with vodka, whiskey, or rum. Just be sure to label the batches so it's clear which one has the booze. When I was fifteen years old, I kept serving myself punch from the wrong pot and was acting a fool!

MAKES 6 TO 8 SERVINGS

1 cup dried
hibiscus flowers

8 cups water

4 apples, cored and
cut in half

1½ cups drained canned
sugarcane in syrup (see
Note), syrup reserved

1 pineapple, peeled,
cored, and cut into slabs
the size of a deck of cards

3 cinnamon sticks

1 pinch fine sea salt

1 cup cane sugar

Rinse the hibiscus flowers under running water for 2 minutes to clean them.

In a large pot, combine the hibiscus, 6 cups of the water, the apples, sugarcane, pineapple, cinnamon sticks, and salt. Set over high heat, partially cover, and bring to a boil. Cook for 30 minutes, then remove from the heat and let sit, covered, for 10 minutes.

Remove and discard the apples; they're too mushy at this point and will ruin the texture. Add the remaining 2 cups water and the sugar and stir to combine. Taste and add some of the sugarcane syrup, if needed, and reheat, if desired.

Set out the pot and let guests ladle the punch into mugs to serve themselves.

NOTES You can find canned sugarcane in large supermarkets or markets that specialize in Asian groceries. The cane looks like bamboo shoots.

To stretch out the punch, simply boil more water with the solids in the pot.

Chocolate

Mexican hot chocolate is traditionally made with cow's milk, but I love it with a creamy nut milk, like macadamia milk. What makes it special is the assortment of spices in the mix. Cinnamon and a bit of cayenne are typical in Mexican hot chocolate, but I borrowed a trick from my mom and also sprinkle in some cardamom, which gives the drink another dimension. This creamy, frothy hot chocolate is not too sweet but so satisfying after a meal. If you have leftover hot chocolate, refrigerate it in an airtight container for up to 3 days, then reheat it with 1 cup water so it doesn't get too thick.

MAKES 4 SERVINGS

5 cups macadamia milk or other creamy nondairy milk

⅓ cup cane sugar

¼ cup cacao powder

⅛ teaspoon ground cardamom

1 pinch cayenne pepper (optional)

2 cinnamon sticks

In a medium saucepan over medium heat, warm ½ cup of the macadamia milk. Add the sugar, cacao powder, cardamom, and cayenne (if using) and stir well with a silicone spatula or a silicone whisk; make sure any lumps are gone and the mixture is thoroughly combined. Add the remaining 4½ cups macadamia milk and cinnamon sticks, turn the heat to medium-low, and simmer for 10 minutes. Remove the cinnamon sticks before serving.

Piña Loca

—◇—

This drink is for sweet-savory lovers. You get the juiciness of pineapple while the jalapeño leans into the "green" flavors of tequila. The pinch of salt really brings it all together. For the best flavor, I prefer a high-quality tequila for this cocktail.

MAKES 1 SERVING

1 large ice cube (optional), plus ice cubes for shaking

6 ounces Agua Fresca de Piña (page 198)

2 ounces blanco tequila

2 dashes aromatic bitters

1 pinch fine sea salt

1 or 2 slices jalapeño

Lime wedge for garnish (optional)

Drop the large ice cube into a rocks glass, if desired.

Fill a cocktail shaker two-thirds of the way with ice, then add the agua fresca, tequila, bitters, and salt. Shake well, about 30 seconds, then strain into the glass. Garnish with the jalapeño slice(s) and lime wedge. Serve right away.

Tomar un Rindo

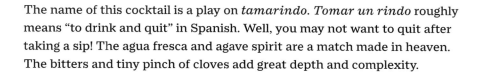

The name of this cocktail is a play on *tamarindo. Tomar un rindo* roughly means "to drink and quit" in Spanish. Well, you may not want to quit after taking a sip! The agua fresca and agave spirit are a match made in heaven. The bitters and tiny pinch of cloves add great depth and complexity.

MAKES I SERVING

1 large ice cube (optional), plus ice cubes for shaking

6 ounces Agua Fresca de Tamarindo (page 199)

2 ounces tequila or mezcal

1 tablespoon fresh lime juice

3 dashes aromatic bitters

1 pinch fine sea salt

Coarsely ground cloves for garnish

Star anise pod for garnish (optional)

Drop the large ice cube into a rocks glass, if desired; or alternatively, chill a martini glass (no ice).

Fill a cocktail shaker two-thirds of the way with ice, then add the agua fresca, tequila, lime juice, bitters, and salt. Shake well, about 30 seconds, then strain into the glass. Garnish with a tiny pinch of ground cloves and a star anise pod, if desired. Serve right away.

Margarita Fuerte

This tamarind margarita was inspired by all my failed recipe attempts for this cookbook. After a long day, I would make this cocktail to sip, and I'd ponder what else I could do to fix the recipes that went wrong. I drank this with my partner, and we sure did enjoy it. "¡Estan muy fuertes!" Boy, are they strong!

MAKES 2 SERVINGS

Coarse salt

½ lime (halved lengthwise), cut into 3 equal wedges, plus the juice of 1 lime

Ice cubes

4 ounces Agua Fresca de Tamarindo (page 199)

4 ounces tequila

8 dashes orange bitters

Pour some coarse salt onto a small plate.

Slice the lime wedges through the middle, stopping before you cut the peel. Place the slit of one wedge on the rim of a highball glass and run it around the rim to moisten. Repeat with a second glass. Dab the rim of each prepared glass in the salt to coat. Fill each glass with ice cubes and perch a remaining lime wedge on each rim, if desired; set aside.

Fill a cocktail shaker two-thirds of the way with ice, then add the agua fresca, tequila, bitters, and lime juice. Shake well, about 30 seconds, then strain into the prepared glasses. Serve right away.

Para Los Agrios

◇

I named this cocktail "Para Los Agrios" ("for the bitters ones") because it has a double dose of tartness from the limeade and lemon juice. Shaking it with aquafaba (liquid from a can of chickpeas) mimics the frothiness you'd get from egg white in a sour.

MAKES 2 SERVINGS

2 large ice cubes or spheres (see Note), plus ice cubes for shaking

4 ounces Pepino y Limón Agua Fresca concentrate (see page 194)

4 ounces gin

3 ounces aquafaba

Juice of 1 lemon

2 maraschino cherries, skewered on picks

Drop the large ice cubes in each of two rocks glasses.

Fill a cocktail shaker two-thirds of the way with ice, then add the concentrate, gin, aquafaba, and lemon juice. Shake vigorously until the aquafaba is frothy, about 2 minutes. Pour, including the foam, into each glass and then drop a maraschino cherry in each glass. Serve right away.

NOTE Serving this cocktail over regular ice cubes will dilute it too much. If you don't have molds to make the larger ice, fill the glasses with ice cubes before you begin making the drink. After shaking the cocktail, dump the ice from the glasses and firmly shake out excess water.

CHAPTER 6

Postrecitos

Some of my earliest memories in the kitchen are of watching mi mama and mi tia baking. I was always hanging around the kitchen when los postrecitos were being made, which was often. In my family, and in most Mexican families, you can never have a complete meal without "the little desserts," whatever the occasion.

When I was a boy, my mother and my aunt never let me help make the desserts. I could only watch and try to steal sugary bites. I can still smell mi tia's almond cookies baking in the oven and recall the sweet nutty flavor and deliciously crumbly texture. At Christmas, our house was filled with the aroma of cinnamon from all the confections being made. The most common treat was arroz con leche, and everyone (including our dogs!) would line up to have some.

As an adult, dessert still makes me happy, especially now that I've learned how to re-create amazing Mexican and Latin American specialties with ingredients that I feel good about. My sweet tooth is satisfied by healthier sweeteners and fats, and desserts that are either whole-grain or gluten-free. Not only are these desserts more nutritious, I think these postrecitos taste even better than the "real" thing.

Desserts bring joy and sweetness to everyday life. These recipes are also a reminder of the importance of celebrations in Mexican culture, and how any occasion can be turned into a fiesta.

Colada de Plátanos

Despite its name, this warm pudding has nothing to do with pina colada. *Colada* means "mixture," and this dessert is a combo of green and ripe plantains. Green plantains are used for the custard; when cooked, they have a starchiness that makes the mixture pudding-like. Then sweet, caramelized ripe plantains, maduros, go on top. This dessert was one of the first things that my partner Gio's mom made for me. I loved it so much that I had to learn how to make it from her!

MAKES 4 TO 6 SERVINGS

2 large or 4 small green plantains

4 cups water

8 ounces piloncillo

2 teaspoons ground cinnamon

1 pinch fine sea salt

Plant-based milk for serving

Maduros (page 136) for topping

In a high-powered blender, combine the plantains, water, piloncillo, cinnamon, and salt and blend on high speed until the mixture is completely smooth, 90 seconds. It's very important that absolutely no lumps remain.

Pour the mixture into a small saucepan over medium heat and bring to a simmer, stirring constantly with a silicone spatula. This part is key, because if you stop stirring, hard lumps will form. Continue to simmer and stir until the mixture becomes thick and sticky, like glue, about 15 minutes; when you lift the spatula, the drip should form a gluey rope. Remove from the heat and let cool for 5 minutes,

Spoon the plantains into individual bowls and then stir in ⅓ to ¼ cup plant-based milk, depending on preference. Top with maduros, and enjoy.

Almond Milk Rice Pudding with Cashew Cream

This recipe is inspired by mi mama's vegan rice pudding. She knew how much I loved arroz con leche, which is traditionally made with cow's milk. So when I came home to visit from college, she surprised me with arroz con leche made with almond milk. It was the first time that she'd made a vegan dish just for me, which really meant a lot.

Adding shredded carrots to arroz con leche was also my mom's idea. It not only makes the dessert more healthful but, along with cinnamon and ginger, gives the rice pudding the flavor of carrot cake. Instead of traditional sweetened condensed milk, I took another cue from my mom and use cashews to thicken the rice pudding and make it extra creamy.

MAKES 8 SERVINGS

½ cup raw cashews

1½ cups water

2 cups uncooked jasmine rice, soaked in water to cover overnight and then drained

3 cups, unsweetened almond milk

¼ teaspoon fine sea salt

3 cinnamon sticks, plus ground cinnamon for sprinkling

1 cup finely grated carrots (optional)

½ teaspoon ground ginger (optional)

¾ cup cane sugar

In a medium pot, cover the cashews with several inches of tap water and boil gently for 20 minutes, then drain.

In a high-powered blender, combine the cashews and ½ cup of the water and blend on high speed until smooth, 30 to 45 seconds. Set this cream aside.

In a large pot over medium heat, combine the rice, almond milk, and remaining 1 cup water; stir in the salt, cinnamon sticks, cashew cream, and the carrots and ground ginger (if using); and bring to a boil. Stir in the sugar, turn the heat to a low simmer, and cook, uncovered, stirring the rice often to make sure it doesn't stick to the bottom of the pan, until the rice is tender and reaches a pudding consistency, 15 to 20 minutes. Remove from the heat and let cool for a few minutes. Remove and discard the cinnamon sticks, if you like.

Sprinkle the rice pudding with ground cinnamon and serve. (It's even better the next day and can be refrigerated for up to 5 days in an airtight container.)

Gelatina de Mango Coco

These layered parfaits are not traditionally Mexican, but they use traditional ingredients. The bottom layer is a mango–coconut milk gelatin. Once that sets, I add a layer of coconut-vanilla cream, which sets up kind of like panna cotta. The tangy-sweet pineapple compote and the sweetened vegan condensed milk on top really take this dish to new heights. You can make the parfaits in 6- to 8-ounce glasses or mason jars to see the layers. They can be refrigerated for up to 3 days.

MAKES 8 SERVINGS

MANGO-COCONUT GELATIN

2 large mangoes, peeled and roughly chopped

One 13-ounce can unsweetened coconut milk

1 cup water

3 tablespoons agave nectar

1 tablespoon plus 1 teaspoon vegan gelatin powder

COCONUT-VANILLA CREAM

One 13-ounce can unsweetened coconut milk

2 tablespoons agave nectar

½ teaspoon pure vanilla extract

1 tablespoon vegan gelatin powder

PINEAPPLE COMPOTE

2 cups chopped pineapple (1 by ½-inch pieces)

1 tablespoon cane sugar

Juice of ½ lemon

Vegan Condensed Milk (page 224) or any other sweetener for topping

To make the mango-coconut gelatin: In a high-powered blender, combine the mangoes, coconut milk, water, agave nectar, and gelatin powder and blend on high speed until super-silky smooth, 45 to 60 seconds. Pour into a small saucepan over medium-low heat and cook for 15 minutes, stirring constantly. The mixture should thicken gradually as it cooks. Remove from the heat and keep stirring but much more slowly until no air bubbles remain, about 5 minutes. It's very important to stir slowly and constantly; stirring too quickly can create more air bubbles.

Using a funnel or turkey baster, divide the mixture evenly among eight glasses or jars (you can use a spoon but it will be messier). Cover and refrigerate until set into a stiff layer, at least 1 hour or up to overnight.

To make the coconut-vanilla cream: In a small saucepan over medium-low heat, combine the coconut milk, agave nectar, vanilla, and gelatin powder and cook, stirring constantly to prevent scorching, for 15 minutes. The mixture will gradually thicken as it cooks. Remove from the heat and let cool for 5 minutes.

Using the funnel or turkey baster, divide the mixture evenly over the mango-coconut gelatin layer in the glasses. Cover and refrigerate until set into a stiff layer, at least 15 minutes. (The higher concentration of gelatin will help it set much more quickly.)

To make the pineapple compote: Meanwhile, in a small saucepan over medium heat, cook the pineapple, stirring constantly to prevent burning, until the liquid released by the pineapple evaporates, about 13 minutes. Stir in the sugar (adding it too soon will not give the liquid a chance to evaporate, and you will end up with more of a pineapple soup than a compote) and lemon juice until combined. Remove from the heat and let cool to room temperature, then refrigerate until chilled, if desired.

Top the parfaits with the compote and vegan condensed milk before serving.

Vegan Condensed Milk

I knew I had to make a vegan version of condensed milk. It's used in so many Mexican desserts, like tres leches cake and rice pudding. This plant-based variation is a great substitute for creamer in coffee and iced coffee. You can also use it in an otherwise traditional horchata, or as a topping for other desserts, like Gelatina de Mango Coco (page 223).

MAKES 4 CUPS

¼ cup warm water

2 tablespoons cornstarch

Two 13.66-ounce cans full-fat coconut milk

1 cup cane sugar or packed light brown sugar

1 tablespoon molasses

1 pinch fine sea salt

In a liquid measuring cup, whisk together the water and cornstarch to form a slurry.

In a medium saucepan over medium heat, combine the coconut milk, sugar, molasses, and salt, then add the slurry, whisk well, and simmer for 10 minutes. Turn the heat to low and cook until very thick, silky, and syrupy, 10 minutes more. Remove from the heat, cover, and let sit for another 10 minutes.

Store the vegan condensed milk in an airtight container in the refrigerator for up to 8 days.

Edgar's No-Bake Mexican Cheesecake

⸺◇⸺

The first time that I brought this dessert to a family gathering, it was for Itzel, a family friend who was eight years old at the time. She has diabetes, so I wanted to make something familiar that didn't have too much sugar. This cheesecake with a raw cashew-based filling was a big hit. Everyone loved it—especially Itzel.

If you've had raw cheesecakes before, you probably know they can be grainy, mostly because the uncooked sugar isn't able to dissolve properly. This one isn't grainy at all! It's super-creamy with already liquid agave nectar, and it has a high proportion of graham cracker crust. I top it with a strawberry compote, which is a bright, tangy complement to the creamy filling. Any leftovers can be refrigerated for up to 5 days.

MAKES ONE 8-INCH CHEESECAKE

CRACKER CRUST

18 vegan graham crackers (2 packets from a 14.4-ounce box)

¼ cup coconut oil, solid but softened (see Note, page 236)

½ teaspoon pure vanilla extract

2 tablespoons unsweetened plant-based milk, at room temperature (I use soy milk)

FILLING

3 cups unsalted raw cashews, soaked in water to cover overnight (or boiled for 15 minutes, then cooled)

⅓ cup cold-pressed virgin coconut oil

¼ cup fresh lemon juice

¼ cup agave nectar (see Note)

1 pinch fine sea salt

½ cup unsweetened plant-based milk (I use soy milk)

STRAWBERRY COMPOTE

1 pound strawberries, hulled and roughly chopped

Juice of 2 lemons

1 tablespoon cane sugar, plus more as needed

To make the crust: Line the bottom and sides of an 8-inch springform pan with parchment paper. Trim off any excess.

Place the graham crackers in a food processor and pulse until small crumbs form. (Alternatively, crush them in a resealable plastic bag with a rolling pin.) Pour the crumbs into the prepared pan and rub in the coconut oil until the mixture is well combined and a uniform texture. Add the vanilla and repeat; then add the plant-based milk and repeat. Using your hands, pack the crumbs into the pan, making sure they reach the edges. Rinse your hands and repeat the packing to be sure every part of the crust is packed down tight. Place the pan in the freezer for 15 minutes.

CONTINUED

To make the filling: Meanwhile, drain the cashews and transfer to a high-powered blender. Add the coconut oil, lemon juice, agave nectar, salt, and plant-based milk and blend on high speed until completely smooth and emulsified, 2½ to 3 minutes. The texture should be thick and creamy and resemble soft-serve ice cream.

Using a rubber spatula, scrape the filling into the chilled crust. Smooth the top and tap the pan firmly on the counter to get rid of air bubbles and smooth out the top even more. Place in the freezer overnight.

To make the compote: In a small saucepan over high heat, combine the strawberries, lemon juice, and sugar and bring to a boil. Then turn the heat to low and simmer until the mixture thickens and the strawberries begin to fall apart, about 10 minutes. Taste and add additional sugar, as needed. Remove from the heat and let cool.

Remove the cheesecake from the freezer, open the springform pan, and unmold; let sit at room temperature for 20 to 25 minutes. Top the cheesecake with the compote and serve.

NOTE For a sweeter cheesecake, substitute *sweetened* plant-based milk or add an additional 2 tablespoons agave nectar.

Galletas de Almendras

Whenever I think about these almond cookies, I think of my Aunt Chely. Galletas de almendras were a fixture at the start of Advent (the weeks leading up to Christmas), and I recall waking up during that time to the aroma of her crushing almonds in the kitchen. This was the only thing that she'd let me help her with, and she's the reason I love baking. My gluten-free version here is a tribute to her original recipe.

It's not just the memories that put me in the holiday mood. The powdered sugar on top of the cookies evokes snowy winters. Now, I dust confectioners' sugar through my grandma's doilies to make patterns on the cookies. She crocheted them for me to use on my future dining table. That touch makes them extra-special, but the cookies are still pretty without the doily patterns.

MAKES 14 TO 16 COOKIES

1 cup whole dry-roasted almonds

2 cups gluten-free all-purpose flour (such as Bob's Red Mill), plus more for dusting

2 teaspoons ground cinnamon

1 teaspoon baking soda

1 teaspoon baking powder

1 pinch fine sea salt

1 cup cane sugar

½ cup coconut oil, melted and cooled, or vegan butter, at room temperature

¼ cup unsweetened plant-based milk, at room temperature

Confectioners' sugar for dusting

Place the almonds in a high-powered blender or food processor and pulse until slightly irregular pieces, double the size of rice grains, form. (Alternatively, chop finely with a knife.) Transfer to a large bowl, then, using a fine-mesh sieve, sift in the flour, cinnamon, baking soda, baking powder, and salt.

In a medium bowl, combine the cane sugar and coconut oil and beat with a fork until blended thoroughly. Add the plant-based milk and beat until the ingredients are uniformly combined. Transfer to the large bowl and use a spoon to mix into the dry ingredients until evenly combined and doughy enough to knead with clean hands. Form the dough into one large ball, then place in a bowl or container, cover, and refrigerate for at least 6 hours (or up to overnight, for best results).

Preheat the oven to 350°F. Line two baking sheets with parchment paper or silicone baking mats.

Remove the dough ball from the refrigerator and let it come to room temperature, about 30 minutes. Dust a work surface with flour and then roll out the dough to about ½ inch thick. Using a 4-inch cookie cutter or a cup, stamp out rounds from the dough and transfer to the prepared baking sheets. Reroll the scraps of dough to stamp out more rounds.

Bake the cookies until lightly browned around the edges, about 12 minutes. Remove them from the baking sheets and transfer to a wire rack. Let cool completely, then dust with confectioners' sugar.

Store the cookies in an airtight container at room temperature for up to 8 days.

Galletas de Jengibre

One of my favorite treats from Mexican pastry shops is marranitos, little gingerbread pigs. My gluten-free ginger cookies are based on marranitos, except these are round and not shaped like pigs. They're flaky outside, chewy inside, and not too sweet. I found that adding a little apple cider vinegar helps make the cookies taste sweet without adding more sugar.

MAKES 16 TO 18 COOKIES

¼ cup water

2 tablespoons ground flaxseed (see Note)

1¾ cups plus 1 tablespoon gluten-free all-purpose flour

1 cup cane sugar

1 teaspoon ground cinnamon

1 teaspoon ground cloves

1 teaspoon baking soda

¼ teaspoon fine sea salt

2 to 3 tablespoons finely chopped peeled ginger (depending on taste preference)

⅓ cup plus 1 tablespoon vegan butter, at room temperature, plus more for greasing (optional)

¼ cup agave nectar

1 teaspoon pure vanilla extract

1 teaspoon apple cider vinegar

In a small cup or bowl, stir together the water and ground flaxseed and let sit until gelatinous, about 10 minutes; this will be the flax "eggs."

Meanwhile, in a large bowl, combine the flour, sugar, cinnamon, cloves, baking soda, and salt and whisk together. In a medium bowl, combine the ginger, vegan butter, agave nectar, vanilla, and vinegar and whisk together. Add the flax "eggs" to the wet ingredients and whisk together well. Pour into the dry ingredients and stir together with a wooden spoon. Refrigerate for 1 hour.

Preheat the oven to 325°F. Grease two baking sheets with vegan butter or line with parchment paper.

Remove the chilled dough from the refrigerator. Using a 2-tablespoon scoop, scoop the dough onto the prepared baking sheets, leaving enough space for the cookies to spread out as they bake. You should have eight or nine cookies on each sheet. Slightly flatten each mound to about 1½ inches in diameter.

Bake the cookies until they have risen a bit and crackled on top, about 15 minutes. Remove them from the baking sheets and transfer to a wire rack. Let cool completely.

Store the cookies in an airtight container at room temperature for up to 8 days.

NOTE If you have whole flaxseed, you can grind them in a blender into a fine powder, then measure out 2 tablespoons.

Sweet Potato Empanadas

Mexican empanadas are sweet and mostly served for dessert, although many people eat them for breakfast with coffee or hot chocolate—and who can blame them? A common flavor is calabaza, or pumpkin, but I was so surprised when I found out that most "pumpkin empanadas" are actually filled with sweet potatoes! I asked one shop owner why and was told it's because pumpkin isn't available throughout the year.

I decided to make mine with sweet potatoes and be transparent about it in the name, although I gave the dough an unconventional tweak. I always felt the crust on traditional empanadas was too pale, so I coat my dough with cinnamon and coconut sugar before baking. When they come out of the oven, they're beautifully browned, crisp, and delicious. The cinnamon and coconut sugar really complement the sweet potatoes (and they'd complement the pumpkin, too, if that's what was actually inside the crust!).

The baked empanadas can be stored in an airtight container in the refrigerator for up to for 7 days, or in the freezer for up to 1 month. To reheat, microwave until warmed through, about 45 seconds.

MAKES 24 TO 26 EMPANADAS

SWEET EMPANADA DOUGH

4 cups all-purpose flour

½ cup cane sugar

1 tablespoon plus 1 teaspoon baking powder

1 teaspoon fine sea salt

1⅓ cups coconut oil, softened but solid (see Note)

1 cup unsweetened plant-based milk, or as needed

FILLING

3 pounds sweet potatoes

¾ cup cane sugar

1 tablespoon ground cinnamon

½ teaspoon ground nutmeg

¼ teaspoon ground ginger

⅛ teaspoon ground cloves

1 pinch fine sea salt

¼ cup packed coconut sugar or brown sugar

1 teaspoon ground cinnamon

¼ cup unsweetened plant-based milk

To make the dough: In a large bowl, combine the flour, sugar, baking powder, and salt and whisk together. Using a butter knife, cut the coconut oil into the flour mixture until well combined and the dough has the texture of fine crumbs.

Sprinkle 1 to 2 tablespoons of the plant-based milk over the dough and mix gently with your hands. Continue to sprinkle the milk on the driest parts of the dough and mix until you can form the dough into a soft uniform ball that's not too sticky or dry. Do not overmix or the dough will get warm and the coconut oil will start to melt! Place the dough ball in a large bowl, cover, and refrigerate for at least 6 hours (or up to overnight for best results).

CONTINUED

To make the filling: Place the sweet potatoes in a large pot, cover with water, and bring to a boil over high heat. Boil until the potatoes are soft and easily pierced with a fork, about 20 minutes. Drain and transfer the sweet potatoes to a large bowl (no need to peel them), then mash with a fork until mostly smooth but still a little chunky. Measure out 2½ cups (reserve the rest for another use—feed to dogs, or use it in another recipe); add the sugar, cinnamon, nutmeg, ginger, cloves, and salt; and stir together until evenly blended. Let cool thoroughly.

Remove the dough ball from the refrigerator and let sit until it comes to room temperature and is malleable and easy to roll, about 20 minutes.

Preheat the oven to 350°F. Line two baking sheets with parchment paper.

Cut the dough into four pieces and form each into a ball. Using a rolling pin, roll out each ball until uniformly thick, about ⅓ inch. Using a 4-inch cookie cutter or a cup, stamp out rounds from the dough and transfer to a baking sheet. Reroll the scraps of dough to stamp out more rounds.

Place a heaping 1 tablespoon of the filling in the center of each round and fold into a half-moon. Using a fork, crimp the edges shut and create the classic empanada appearance.

On a plate, combine the coconut sugar and cinnamon. Brush the outside of each empanada with the plant-based milk and gently dab in the cinnamon-sugar to thinly coat all around. Transfer to the prepared baking sheets, spacing the empanadas apart.

Bake the empanadas until the crusts are golden brown and crisp all over, about 20 minutes; you will smell when the empanadas are ready. Let them cool a bit before serving—unless you can't wait!

NOTE The coconut oil should be solid but malleable—at room temperature on a temperate day is ideal.

Apple Empanadas

Think of these empanadas as little apple hand pies. You can use the dough from the Sweet Potato Empanadas, then fill and bake them the same way. Just as with the sweet potato version, the cinnamon–coconut sugar coating makes them extra tasty!

The baked empanadas can be stored in an airtight container in the refrigerator for up to for 7 days, or in the freezer for up to 1 month. To reheat, microwave until warmed through, about 45 seconds.

MAKES 20 TO 24 EMPANADAS

FILLING

5 Granny Smith apples, peeled, cored, and diced

½ cup cane sugar

2 teaspoons all-purpose flour

1½ teaspoons ground cinnamon

1 tablespoon fresh lemon juice

1 pinch fine sea salt

Sweet Empanada Dough (see page 235)

¼ cup packed coconut sugar or brown sugar

1 teaspoon ground cinnamon

¼ cup unsweetened plant-based milk

To make the filling: In a small saucepan over medium heat, combine the apples, sugar, flour, cinnamon, lemon juice, and salt and cook, stirring occasionally, until the apples are tender, 10 to 12 minutes. Let cool thoroughly.

Remove the dough ball from the refrigerator and let sit until it comes to room temperature and is malleable and easy to roll, about 20 minutes.

Preheat the oven to 350°F. Line two baking sheets with parchment appear.

Cut the dough into four pieces and form each into a ball. Using a rolling pin, roll out each ball until uniformly thick, about ⅓ inch. Using a 4-inch cookie cutter or a cup, stamp out rounds from the dough and transfer to a baking sheet. Reroll the scraps of dough to stamp out more rounds.

Place a heaping 1 tablespoon of the filling in the center of each round and fold into a half-moon. Using a fork, crimp the edges shut and create the classic empanada appearance.

On a plate, combine the coconut sugar and cinnamon. Brush the outside of each empanada with the plant-based milk and gently dab in the cinnamon-sugar to thinly coat all around. Transfer to the prepared baking sheets, spacing the empanadas apart.

Bake the empanadas until the crusts are golden brown and crisp all over, about 20 minutes; you will smell when the empanadas are ready. Let them cool a bit before serving—unless you can't wait!

Pastelitos

I made these cakes as mini Bundts so you can have them anytime, with just a few people or even by yourself. I also took care to make them diabetes-friendly. I get sad when I see some of my relatives unable to partake in desserts. I want everyone to still be able to indulge in something sweet, so I had them in mind when choosing the ingredients for this recipe. For example, the oat and almond flours have more protein and fiber than wheat flour. Both aspects can slow the absorption of sugar and help improve blood sugar levels for those with type 2 diabetes.

**MAKES 4 MINI
BUNDT CAKES**

Coconut oil for greasing

¼ cup water

2 tablespoons chia seeds

½ cup unsweetened almond milk

2 tablespoons apple cider vinegar or lemon juice

1 cup thick vegan yogurt

½ cup agave nectar

1 teaspoon vanilla paste or extract

1½ cups oat flour

1½ cups almond flour

1 teaspoon baking soda

½ teaspoon fine sea salt

Vegan frosting for topping

Crushed freeze-dried raspberries for topping (optional)

Preheat the oven to 350°F. Grease four 4-inch Bundt pans with coconut oil. (Alternatively, grease one 9-inch Bundt pan; see Note). Set aside.

In a large bowl, stir together the water and chia seeds and let sit until gelatinous, about 10 minutes; this will be the chia "eggs." Meanwhile, in a liquid measuring cup, stir together the almond milk and vinegar and let sit for 10 minutes. (By the time the chia "eggs" are ready, this will be ready as well.)

Pour the almond milk mixture into the chia "eggs"; add the yogurt, agave nectar, and vanilla; and whisk together. Sift in both flours, the baking soda, and salt and stir together, just until well combined. Divide the batter equally among the prepared pans.

Bake the cakes until the tops are browned and a toothpick inserted close to the center comes out clean, 35 to 40 minutes. Remove from the oven and let cool in the pans for 15 minutes. Invert each pan onto a plate and tap gently to dislodge the cake. (At this point, you can store the cakes in an airtight container at room temperature for up to 7 days.)

Serve the cakes topped with vegan frosting and freeze-dried raspberries, if desired.

NOTE If using a 9-inch Bundt pan, the baking time will be 50 to 55 minutes.

Acknowledgments

I want to thank my family who have supported me throughout my life. To my mama, you have been the rock that I needed while growing up. As I was writing this book, you often were the one tasting my food and giving everything an amazing review. To my abuelita, of course, you have been an amazing supporter of my cookbook. To my partner, Giovanny, you helped me through everything and were also my last-minute assistant when I needed someone the most. You were a recipe tester and someone who helped me so much emotionally. Love you so much! My tias Lupita, Chely, Belsa, and Evelia, and Gio's mom, Marleny, helped me with some recipes. Los quiero mucho. My sister and her boyfriend, Tre, tasted all of my food and gave it constructive criticism.

Thank you to my friends, who are basically extended family, especially Grace Joseph. You were my assistants for the cookbook. I want to thank Anna Kenney for helping as well, and for the photograph on the title page. I love you and appreciate you both. I also want to thank Deborah Lustig, you've helped me through the toughest times and have supported my dream to write a cookbook. Much love to you and your family. Te queiro mucho.

Thank you to my friends from social media, a lot of whom I haven't met in person but truly mean the world to me. You inspire me, you push me, and you are there when I need you. I want to especially thank Jasmine from @sweetsimplevegan and Chris from @consciouschris for trying out my recipes; Joanne @thekoreanvegan for always being my biggest fan, I have so much love for you; Nisha from @rainbowplantlife for being the sweetest person and for always sharing the love with me;

Maria @foodbymaria for always keeping it real and for being my friend even though I'm a weirdo; and Zuliya from @naturallyzuzu for always sending your love and amazing support on social media. I don't know where I would be without any of you.

Thank you to Julie from @gomethodology. You have always supported me with everything you can think of, from advice to giving praise. I couldn't be any happier to be your photographer and am so pleased to have connected online with you while I was still in college. And to MaryMar @mmclay for the beautiful ceramics shown in these photographs. Over the years I've purchased your whole series of ceramics, and no regrets there!

Thank you to my agent, Leigh Eisenman, for always keeping me on task and reminding me that I am amazing and to stay focused, especially during the pandemic. And to my writer, Susan Choung, for being such an amazing person and being able to get my thoughts to be clear and to have a story that is organized. You rock!

Thank you as well to my team at Ten Speed Press, especially my awesome editor Dervla Kelly, production editor Doug Ogan, designer Lisa Bieser, production manager Dan Myers, Brianne Sperber in marketing, David Hawk in publicity, and editorial assistant Zoey Brandt.

Finally, it's all thanks to the people who follow my journey on social media that I have been able to create this amazing cookbook. If you're reading this, just know I am sending you so many hugs and kisses. I appreciate you from the bottom of my heart.

About the Authors

EDGAR CASTREJÓN is a chef, recipe developer, food stylist, and photographer based in the San Francisco Bay Area. While in school studying plant science and nutrition, he launched his Instagram account @edgarraw, where these days his followers tune in for his creative, nourishing, plant-based recipes and beautiful food photography.

SUSAN CHOUNG is a cookbook writer, editor, and recipe tester. She was formerly the books editor at *Food & Wine* for many years. Born in South Korea, Susan was raised in Brooklyn, New York, where she worked at her parents' Italian and Jewish delis. She still has strong opinions about sandwiches.

Index

Copyright © 2021 by Edgar Castrejón.

All rights reserved.
Published in the United States by Ten Speed Press, an imprint of Random House,
a division of Penguin Random House LLC, New York.
www.tenspeed.com

Ten Speed Press and the Ten Speed Press colophon are registered trademarks
of Penguin Random House LLC.

Library of Congress Cataloging-in-Publication Data
    Names: Castrejon, Edgar, author. | Choung, Susan, author.
    Title: Provecho : 100 vegan Mexican recipes to celebrate culture and
        community / Edgar Castrejon with Susan Choung.
    Description: Emeryville : Ten Speed Press, 2021.
    Identifiers: LCCN 2020053110 (print) | LCCN 2020053111 (ebook) |
        ISBN 9781984859112 (hardcover) | ISBN 9781984859129 (ebook)
    Subjects: LCSH: Cooking—New Mexico. | Vegetarian cooking. |
        Cooking (Natural foods). | LCGFT: Cookbooks.
    Classification: LCC TX715 .C4275 2021 (print) | LCC TX715 (ebook) |
        DDC 641.5972—dc23
    LC record available at https://lccn.loc.gov/2020053110
    LC ebook record available at https://lccn.loc.gov/2020053111

Hardcover ISBN: 978-1-9848-5911-2
eBook ISBN: 978-1-9848-5912-9

Printed in China

Editor: Dervla Kelly | Production editor: Doug Ogan
Designer: Lisa Schneller Bieser | Art directors: Kelly Booth and Betsy Stromberg
Production designers: Mari Gill and Faith Hague
Production manager: Dan Myers | Prepress color manager: Jane Chinn
Copyeditor: Amy Kovalski | Proofreader: Amy Bauman | Indexer: Ken DellaPenta
Publicist: David Hawk | Marketer: Brianne Sperber

10 9 8 7 6 5 4 3 2 1

First Edition